Cambridge Ele

Elements in International Economics
edited by
Kenneth A. Reinert
George Mason University

INTERNATIONAL INVESTMENT INCOME

Joseph P. Joyce
Wellesley College

CAMBRIDGE
UNIVERSITY PRESS

Shaftesbury Road, Cambridge CB2 8EA, United Kingdom

One Liberty Plaza, 20th Floor, New York, NY 10006, USA

477 Williamstown Road, Port Melbourne, VIC 3207, Australia

314–321, 3rd Floor, Plot 3, Splendor Forum, Jasola District Centre,
New Delhi – 110025, India

103 Penang Road, #05–06/07, Visioncrest Commercial, Singapore 238467

Cambridge University Press is part of Cambridge University Press & Assessment,
a department of the University of Cambridge.

We share the University's mission to contribute to society through the pursuit
of education, learning and research at the highest international levels of excellence.

www.cambridge.org
Information on this title: www.cambridge.org/9781009613446

DOI: 10.1017/9781009613392

First published 2025

A catalogue record for this publication is available from the British Library

ISBN 978-1-009-61344-6 Hardback
ISBN 978-1-009-61340-8 Paperback
ISSN 2753-9326 (online)
ISSN 2753-9318 (print)

Cambridge University Press & Assessment has no responsibility for the persistence
or accuracy of URLs for external or third-party internet websites referred to in this
publication and does not guarantee that any content on such websites is, or will
remain, accurate or appropriate.

International Investment Income

Elements in International Economics

DOI: 10.1017/9781009613392
First published online: February 2025

Joseph P. Joyce
Wellesley College

Author for correspondence: Joseph P. Joyce, jjoyce@wellesley.edu

Abstract: International investments yield returns in the forms of multinational profits, dividends and interest on equity and debt, and the charges on bank loans. These payments are recorded in the current account of the balance of payments and constitute a significant component of many countries' current accounts. Foreign direct investment (FDI)-generated income is often channeled by firms through countries with low tax rates and regulations. Emerging markets regularly have large FDI income deficits, but a substantial portion of these payments are reinvested. Portfolio securities provide income from diversified securities and lower risk. Global banking offers financing from foreign sources, which may support stability during periods of domestic crises.

Keywords: international investments, current account, primary account, FDI, portfolio equity and debt

ISBNs: 9781009613446 (HB), 9781009613408 (PB), 9781009613392 (OC)
ISSNs: 2753-9326 (online), 2753-9318 (print)

Contents

1 International Investment Income

1.1 International Investment Income and BOP

Globalization is the product of the integration of markets across borders, including financial flows as well as trade in goods and services and the migration of labor. The inflows and outflows of these movements are recorded in the balance of payments, which records a country's transactions with the rest of the world. In the case of financial flows, these investments can yield income in the forms of profits, dividends and interest payments, and bank fees. Those flows also appear in the balance of payments.

International transactions are measured through the use of double-entry bookkeeping, an accounting method. This system was first developed in the fifteenth century by banks and firms in Italy (Mills 1994). Each transaction is recorded as a credit or debit to fulfill the accounting requirement:

$$\text{Assets} \ = \ \text{Liabilities} \ + \ \text{Equity} \tag{1}$$

These transactions are recorded in the balance of payments, which was developed during the age of mercantilism. Mercantilism, an economic doctrine developed in the sixteenth century, assumed that a country's wealth included its holdings of precious metals, particularly gold (Reinert 2021). A country received gold when it had more exports than imports and the surplus was settled through an inflow of gold from the economy with a deficit. The balance of trade, a component of the balance of payments, was used to track these payments.

Mercantilism fell out of favor in the eighteenth century after criticism by economists such as David Hume and Adan Smith, and the balance of payments received less attention. It regained its usefulness in the nineteenth century as international trade and financial flows rose in importance (High 2000). The first versions of the balance of payments were calculated in that period as more data regarding international transactions were recorded. The League of Nations published balance of payments statistics during the interwar period, in part to establish a common accounting framework that could be used to compare the balance of payments of different countries (Badger 1951). The IMF took over this task after World War II. The rules for recording transactions in the balance of payments are periodically revised and updated.

Table 1 shows the modern balance of payments (BOP), which has three components: the current account (CUR), the capital account (CAP), and the financial account (FIN):

$$\text{BOP} \ = \ \text{CUR} \ + \ \text{CAP} \ + \ \text{FIN} \tag{2}$$

Table 1 Balance of payments

Balance of Payments	Credits	Debits
Current Account		
Balance of Trade		
Primary Income		
Compensation of Employees		
Investment Income		
Direct Investment		
Portfolio Investment		
Other Investment		
Reserve Assets		
Other Primary Income		
Secondary Income		
Capital Account		
Financial Account		
Direct Investment		
Portfolio Investment		
Financial Derivatives		
Other Investment		
Reserve Assets		
Net Errors and Omissions		

Source: IMF (2013)

The current account measures international trade, primary income that is derived from productive factors, and secondary income arising from transfers. The financial account records transactions in financial assets, and the capital account registers nonfinancial asset transactions. (The IMF uses a different methodology to record the acquisition of assets and liabilities.) Each of those items includes credits and debits that can be utilized to calculate the net flows of each of the components, which show a surplus or deficit. While the overall balance of payments must balance due to double entry bookkeeping, the individual components may show surpluses or deficits that offset the net flows of the other components.

1.2 Current Account

Table 1 also includes the separate components of the current account, which include the balance of trade (BOT), primary income (PRI), and secondary income (SEC):

$$CUR = BOT + PRI + SEC \tag{3}$$

The trade balance records exports and imports of goods and services. Primary income consists of the income received for providing productive resources, including the payments to resident workers from foreign firms and payments to foreign workers from domestic firms (LAB), receipts and payments on financial holdings (INV), and payments for the use of natural resources (NAT):

$$PRI = LAB + INV + NAT \tag{4}$$

For most countries, returns on investments exceed the other sources of primary income.

Investment income includes the earnings on foreign direct investment undertaken by multinational firms (DIR), dividends and interest payments on portfolios of equity and debt (POR), and a "other" category (OTH) that keeps track of payments for international banks among other items. There are also the earnings that a country's central bank earns on its reserve holdings (RES).

$$INV = DIR + POR + OTH + RES \tag{5}$$

Net secondary income is the last category in the current account, and it includes the transfer of funds, either between private residents (TRP) or governments (TRG).

$$SEC = TRP + TRG \tag{6}$$

Table 2 shows the net current accounts and its components for Brazil and the United States in 2022. Brazil recorded a current account deficit of $48,253 million, despite achieving surpluses in its balance of trade and secondary income. The deficit in primary income ($56,530 million), which was due to the substantial deficits in direct investment income ($34.792 million) and portfolio income payments ($20,650 million), greatly exceeded those surpluses.

The United States also had a current account deficit of $1,012,103 million, but its deficit was due to its trade deficit of $944,770 million. This amount was partly offset by a net primary income surplus of $115,961 million, largely due to net investment income of $154,151 million. This surplus reflected net receipts of income from direct investments abroad of $288,748 million, which was partly offset by a deficit in net payments on portfolio equity and debt of $157,573 million. US-based multinationals received large amounts of income from their foreign subsidiaries (Section 3), while the United States obtains funds from the rest of the world by issuing stocks and bonds.

Table 2 Current accounts: Brazil, United States (2022)

	Brazil (million $)	United States (million $)
Current Account	−48,253	−1,012,103
Balance of Trade	4,536	−944,770
Primary Income	−56,530	115,961
Compensation of Employees	101	−17,379
Investment Income	−56,631	154,151
Direct Investment Income	−34,792	288,748
Portfolio Investment Income	−20,650	−129,681
Other Income	−7374	−27,892
Reserve Assets	6,181	2,165
Other Primary Income	0	0
Secondary Income	3,742	−183,294

Source: IMF, *Balance of Payments Statistics*

Net investment income flows vary greatly among countries. Figure 1 shows the countries with the largest surpluses in 2022. These were recorded in Japan ($263.885 million), the United States ($164,602 million), Germany ($160,745 million), and France ($48,892 million).

Figure 2 shows the countries with the largest deficits. These include China (−$203,140 million), Ireland (−$150,727 million), Australia (−$73,949 million), and Brazil (−$61,998 million).

The net flows depend largely on a country's international investment position. Table 3 lists the components of the stock of foreign financial assets held by domestic residents and the domestic liabilities owned by their foreign counterparts.

To calculate the net international investment position (NIIP) the latter is subtracted from the former; a nation with a positive (negative) NIIP is a creditor (debtor) nation.

> Foreign assets owned by domestic residents
> − Domestic assets owned by foreign residents   (7)
> = Net International Investment Position (Creditor $(+)$/ Debtor $(-)$)

The United States, which borrowed extensively in the nineteenth century to finance its own development, became a creditor nation after World War I and retained that position until 1989, when government borrowing pushed the country into debtor status. By the end of 2023, the United States had a net

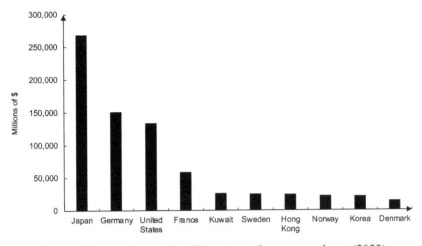

Figure 1 Largest international investment income surpluses (2022)

Source: IMF, *Balance of Payments Statistics*

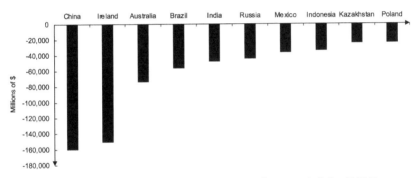

Figure 2 Largest international investment income deficits (2022)

Source: IMF, *Balance of Payments Statistics*

external position of −$19.8 trillion, which represented about 72% of its GDP. Japan, on the other hand, is a net creditor with more foreign assets owned by Japanese residents and firms than foreigners hold in Japan, and its NIIP in 2023 was $3.5 trillion, equal to about 71% of its economy. The NIIP status of emerging market countries differ: China is a net creditor (13% of its GDP), while Brazil is a debtor (−40% of GDP).

Usually we expect countries with positive (negative) NIIPs to have positive (negative) investment income flows. However, both France and the United States had had negative NIIPs in recent years but surpluses in their net investment incomes. The reason for this anomaly lies in how the income is generated. Investment income depends not only on a country's stocks of assets and

Table 3 International investment position

Assets	Liabilities
Direct Investment of domestic firms	Direct Investment of foreign firms
Portfolio investment of residents	Portfolio investment of foreign residents
Financial Derivatives of residents	Financial Derivatives of foreign residents
Other investments of residents	Other investments of foreign residents
Reserve Assets of central bank	

Source: IMF (2013)

liabilities, but also on the returns earned or paid on these. A higher return received from the assets than the yield paid on the liabilities can offset the larger amount of liabilities, and result in an income surplus (Section 3).

1.3 GDP vs GNI vs GNDI

In open economies, there is a divergence between Gross Domestic Product (GDP), the value of all final goods and services produced within a country, and Gross National Income (GNI), the value of all final goods and services produced with a country's productive resources, either domestically or in another country. Primary income, the net value of the international payments of the factors of production, records the difference between the two measurements:

$$\text{GNI} = \text{GDP} + \text{PRI} \tag{8}$$

In a closed economy the two aggregates are equal, but open economies have primary income surpluses and deficits. For most countries the difference between the two is relatively small, but in some countries with significant international activity, there can be a gap between domestic output and the value of domestic and foreign activities.

Ireland, for example, is the host for many multinational firms that have manufacturing and other facilities located there. Among the firms with local affiliates are Google, IBM, Medtronic, and Dell. These local units are profitable, in part because of Ireland's low corporate tax rate (Section 3). Their profits are recorded as debits in investment income and the primary balance, which results in GNI per capita lower than GDP per capita. The differences can be relatively significant: in 2022, for example, Ireland's per capita GDP of 98,745 Euros greatly surpassed per capita GNI of 70,913 Euros.

But the inequality can go the other way. Kuwait has a large oil surplus and invests part of the proceeds in foreign firms, financial institutions, and governments. This extra income pushes GNI per capita above GDP per capita. The difference is not as stark as in Ireland, but 2022's GNI per capita was 15% greater than its GDP per capita.

An analysis of a country's domestic income based solely on GNI would not include the value of the net transfers that are recorded in the secondary income balance. The net flows can be used to derive another macro aggregate: Gross National Disposable Income (GNDI):

$$\text{GNDI} = \text{GDP} + \text{PRI} + \text{SEC} \tag{9}$$

For countries that receive relatively large amounts of remittances, such as Liberia and Haiti, the extra amount of income included in the GNDI can be considerable.

1.4 Current Account Adjustment

Most analyses of the current account focus on the trade balance and ignore primary and secondary income. The standard policy prescription response to an unsustainable current account deficit includes an exchange rate depreciation to facilitate expenditure switching from imports to exports and contractionary macro policies to induce expenditure reduction. However, the growth in the size of primary income, largely due to investment income, has shown that current account deficits can no longer be attributed solely to trade deficits. There are countries where primary income deficits have exceeded trade deficits and dominated the current account, including Brazil, Colombia, and South Africa (Forbes, Hjortsoe, and Nenova 2017). Moreover, in most countries, the current account balance has a large and positive correlation with the trade balance. Primary income, on the other hand, is negatively correlated with the trade balance (Colacelli, Gautam, and Rebillard 2021). Wacker (2024) points out that income balances are much more persistent than the trade balances, and therefore an assessment of a country's current account imbalance should differentiate between deficits due to the income balance and those reflecting a trade deficit.

The exchange rate has a direct impact on domestic value of the income balance. In the case of a country with assets denominated in a foreign currency but liabilities denominated in the domestic currency, an exchange rate depreciation will raise the value of the income credits while lowering the value of the income debits. The domestic value of foreign currency denominated assets will increase. The exchange rate change can also affect the values of the assets and liabilities in the NIIP. The domestic value of foreign currency denominated assets will increase. But if the liabilities are also denominated in the foreign currency, then a depreciation will raise the value of both, with the net effect depending on the amounts and denomination of the assets and liabilities (Bénétrix, Lane, and Shambaugh 2015).

There are numerous linkages between the current account and the NIIP, on the one hand, and the trade balance and primary income on the other (Alberola, Estrada, and Viani 2020). Investment income surpluses (deficits), for example, improve (worsen) the current account, which allows a country to invest (borrow) more abroad through the financial account, which in turn further increases (decreases) the NIIP. But a negative NIIP can provide a positive income flow if the return on a country's assets exceeds the yield paid on its liabilities. Moreover, a change in the NIIP may have a wealth effect, as an increasing (decreasing) position allows may lead to an increase (decrease) in the demand for foreign goods and a deterioration (improvement) in the current account via the trade balance. The overall effect of the two linkages is an empirical issue, which has been investigated in several recent papers.

Alberola, Estrada, and Viani (2020), for example, report that trade balance changes in debtor countries contribute to current account adjustment and offset income balances that tend to worsen the current account. Colacelli, Gautam, and Rebillard (2021) find that in the case of Japan an appreciation of the real exchange rate on net income reinforces the change in the trade balance. However, the trade balance change is more significant in the adjustment of the current account than the income balance. Eugster and Donato (2022) find that an appreciation of the Swiss real exchange rate has a negative but short-run effect on the trade balance that is offset by a positive effect on investment income. Behar and Hassan (2022), who aggregate primary and secondary income, show that the exchange rate has similar effects on income credits and debits, which cancel each other out and therefore are not important in current account adjustment.

Donato and Tille (2024) find that the impact of an exchange rate change on investment income depends in part on the measurement of the exchange rate. In the case of a country's bilateral exchange rate with the US dollar, there is only an impact on the payments of FDI and portfolio debt and both receipts and payments on other investments. However, an appreciation of the broadly defined exchange rate has stronger results, with an appreciation of the dollar reducing yields on both receipts and payments.

Current account adjustment, therefore, is more complicated if a substantial portion of a current account deficit stems from a primary income deficit. The change in the trade balance that follows an exchange rate depreciation will not have the same effect on the primary balance. In addition, the primary balance is more persistent than the trade balance, thus slowing any correction in the current account.

1.5 Summary

The returns on foreign investments have grown over time and have become significant components of the current account of the balance of payments. International income includes the profits of multinational firms, dividends and interest on portfolio holdings of foreign equity and debt, and other forms of income, most significantly from bank activities. Central banks also receive income from their holdings of foreign reserve assets. These flows distinguish GDP from GNI, and in some countries, the difference is considerable.

An assessment of the current account should differentiate among the components of the current account. The role of the primary balance in correcting a current account deficit is uncertain. The primary balance is more persistent than the trade balance, and the response to an exchange rate depreciation depends on several characteristics, including the currency composition of the external assets and liabilities.

2 History of International Investment Income

2.1 First Era of Globalization

Records exist of the use of financial instruments in the earliest societies (Goetzmann 2017). Finance allowed the Mesopotamian civilizations, for example, to incorporate time into the planning of production and trade to mitigate risk. Clay tablets were used to record loans and the interest to be paid by the borrower. Similarly, credit systems evolved in China as agriculture and business expanded, and the government in some cases placed limits on the interest that could be placed on loans.

In later periods, religions, including Judaism, Christianity, and Islam, condemned the practice of usury, that is, the charging of interest on loans. Over time exceptions were allowed, and eventually Christians and Jews were allowed to make loans with interest payments. Banks in Renaissance Italy avoided the usury restrictions by trading bills of exchange that facilitated commerce. Usury laws were later used to place limits on the maximum interest rate that could be charged on loans.

Dividends paid by business firms are a more recent innovation. The first business organizations that bear resemblance to today's multinationals were the British East India Company, founded in 1600, and the Dutch East India Company (VOC), founded in 1602. Both were set up to administer trade activities in Asia. The VOC paid the first dividend in 1610 in the form of spices. The first cash dividend paid by the VOC was issued in 1612.

Financial depth was limited in Europe at the beginning of the nineteenth century. However, there were forces that led to accelerations in finance as well as trade and migration. Improved transportation on land (railroads) and sea (iron-hulled steam ships) enabled dependable trade flows and safer and cheaper migration, which led to profitable investment opportunities. Expanded communications methods (telegraph, telephone, cable) allowed producers to follow their products to their markets while investors could keep track of their funds in foreign locations. Great Britain, the global hegemon, generally maintained peaceful conditions. All these conditions coalesced around 1870, which is usually given as the start of the First Age of Globalization (Findlay and O'Rourke 2007) (Section 7).

The Gold Standard was also adopted by many countries at this time. This monetary system gave confidence to investors in the value of their money when they invested in foreign assets (Obstfeld and Taylor 2004). The Gold Standard linked a country's money supply to the amount of gold held by the central bank, which would exchange paper money to gold and vice versa. This commitment effectively linked together currency exchange rates.

The Gold Standard was one of the elements of the Mundell-Fleming "trilemma" that governed international monetary systems (Mundell 1963). The trilemma maintained that a country could have two, but only two of these characteristics:

1. Unregulated capital flows;
2. Fixed exchange rate;
3. Independent monetary policy.

By adopting the Gold Standard, a country renounced the ability to use monetary policy for domestic goals. Investors faced no limitations on their ability to move money around the globe without government interference, confident in the maintenance of the purchasing power of their funds.

Great Britain, as the predominant power, was the major source of funds for foreign investment during this period. The flow of net foreign investment averaged about 4.3% of British GNP between 1870 and 1914 (Edelstein 1982). As a result, British net foreign assets rose in value from about 7% of the stock of national wealth in 1850 to 14% in 1870 and 32% in 1913. Most of these assets consisted of bonds issued by foreign governments or firms, and in many cases, the recipient countries were part of the British Empire or were Dominion countries, such as Canada, Australia, and New Zealand. The United States also received a large proportion of British capital flows, including in the form of bonds issued by US railroads.

There were also businesses that operated across frontiers (Jones 2005), taking advantage of the same developments – better travel and communications – that fostered trade. These were successors to the European trading companies of the seventeenth and eighteenth centuries. The business operations that took place in the nineteenth and early twentieth centuries took different organizational forms, including "free-standing" firms that did not have a parent unit but collaborated with other similar firms.

France was also a major international investor during this period. French capital flows, unlike the British, were not directed to their colonies, and much of this investment was allocated to Russia, the Balkan countries and Latin America (Graff, Kenwood, and Lougheed 2014). German and US foreign investment also increased in this period, and direct investment accounted for a significant proportion of the US flows.

Foreign investments were profitable for their investors. The rates of return on foreign portfolio investments held in European countries were usually higher than those from domestic investments. One study estimated that the returns in Great Britain from foreign investments yielded 5.7% versus 4.6% on domestic investments during the period of 1870 and 1913 (Edelstein 1976). The reasons for the gap included the high returns available in the relatively underdeveloped foreign regions. Much of the foreign investment established linkages between industrial Europe and periphery nations that were the source of commodities. The investment income that Britain and other European capital exporters received was sufficient to cover trade balance deficits and leave funds for further export (Salter 1951; Graff, Kenwood, and Lougheed 2014).

In 1920, John Maynard Keynes, who had been a member of the British delegation to the post–World War I conference at Versailles, wrote about the consequences of the treaty that had been imposed on Germany by the victors. He gave an elegiac view of how globalization had affected British citizens before the war, and included references to foreign finance (Keynes 1920):

> The inhabitant of London could order by telephone, sipping his morning tea in bed, the various products of the whole earth, in such quantity as he might see fit, and reasonably expect their early delivery upon his doorstep; he could at the same moment and by the same means adventure his wealth in the natural resources and new enterprises of any quarter of the world, and share, without exertion or even trouble, in their prospective fruits and advantages; or he could decide to couple the security of his fortunes with the good faith of the townspeople of any substantial municipality in any continent that fancy or information might recommend.

But not all European citizens enjoyed the benefits of the new foreign enterprises. The ownership of financial assets was concentrated in wealthy households in Europe in the pre–World War I period (Piketty 2014). Records of household estates in Great Britain and France provide evidence of increasing amounts of foreign assets held by the upper-income classes. These yielded incomes that allowed the wealthy to accumulate more assets, reinforcing the inequalities in wealth and income.

2.2 Interwar Period

The onset of World War I put an abrupt end to the unimpeded flows of goods, people, and money across national borders, as well as the prosperity that accompanied them. Private capital flows contracted, and the assets of firms of enemy nations were confiscated by governments. Exchange controls were increasingly used to restrict monetary flows. Great Britain and other nations came off the Gold Standard, which allowed their governments more latitude in financing the war. The United States maintained convertibility but embargoed gold exports.

The end of the war seemed to open a return to the prewar prosperity, at least for those who benefited from the prewar order. But the war effort imposed significant costs. Much of Britain's gold and foreign assets were exhausted, and the government had incurred a massive amount of debt to finance its expenditures. France also lost assets, including the value of its Russian securities when the Bolsheviks came to power. Similarly, Germany had depleted its holdings of foreign securities. It has been estimated that these three countries lost assets of over $12 billion, one-third of the investments they had accumulated in the previous century (Feinstein 1995). US investments also fell (Lipsey 2003). The loss of these assets meant the loss of the international income that had benefited their affluent citizens.

Many governments sought to return to the foundations of the order that had prevailed before 1914, including a restoration of the Gold Standard and a resumption of capital flows. But the hardships imposed by the war had overturned the willingness of the people who had suffered so much to accept prewar wages and prices (Eichengreen and Temin 2000). The British government reverted to the Gold Standard in 1925, but it was impossible to go back to the 1914 prices and wages that had propped it up. The extra strains of the Great Depression forced Britain to abandon the Gold Standard for a second time in 1931. The United States followed, with President Roosevelt taking the United States off the Gold Standard in 1932. The need to arrest the severe economic downturns dominated any possible return to the Gold Standard or open capital accounts.

Private capital flows resumed during the 1920s (Solimano and Watts 2005; Accominotti and Eichengreen 2016). The United States emerged as the major financial center and a net creditor nation, with New York taking on the role of "banker to the world." Capital flows originated in New York and in many cases portfolio loans were destined for European governments. By 1929, the value of US portfolio investment abroad exceeded its direct investments for the first time (Lipsey 2003).

However, the Great Depression shut down private financial activity. Long-term capital flows ceased while speculative short-term flows responded to anticipated changes in government policies and exchange rate pegs. Controls on capital flows and exchange rates proliferated, as did commercial measures designed to limit imports. The exchange controls blocked the cross-border repatriation of profits to asset owners, which forced some firms to reinvest their earnings in the host nations (Jones 2005).

World War II further deepened the divisions among countries. Governments sequestered the domestic assets of enemy nations. Trade and capital flows, already restricted by tariffs and capital controls, were further impeded by the need for governments to furnish and pay for armaments and other war-related materials. The war devastated the stock of FDI in Germany and Japan. The Soviet Union's subsequent occupation of Eastern Europe and the Chinese Communist takeover of that country essentially removed those countries from the financial structure of the global economy.

2.3 Second Era of Globalization

In 1944, the representatives of forty-four nations met in Bretton Woods, a New Hampshire resort, to plan the postwar international economic regime. One goal they shared was their intent to avoid the instability of the prewar period that had contributed to political chaos. The new international monetary regime, called the Bretton Woods system, obliged members to peg their currencies in terms of dollars or gold. The International Monetary Fund (IMF) was established to help member nations deal with external sector imbalances without engaging in competitive exchange rate depreciations.

Since short-term capital flows were viewed as destabilizing, Article VI of the IMF's Articles of Agreement gave member countries the right to "regulate international capital movements." This was a different response to the policy trilemma than that of the previous era of globalization. Governments acquired the ability to use monetary policy for domestic goals, such as full employment, in exchange for surrendering the openness of the capital account. In view of the experience with prewar capital flows, this was seen as a sensible trade-off.

However, Article VIII mandated the convertibility of currencies for all current account movements, including payments on international investment income (Elizalde 2008). Governments could delay or bar new capital flows, but they could not suspend the income generated by existing investments. Article XIV also gave the IMF's members the ability to delay accepting the provisions of Article VIII. It took several years for European governments to have the capability to accept the obligations of Article VIII, but by 1958 France, Italy, West Germany, and the United Kingdom declared their currencies convertible for current account transactions.

Capital restrictions were generally maintained during the Bretton Woods era, but there was a gradual relaxation of some controls in advanced economies. One development during the 1950s that contributed to the decontrol of capital flows was the emergence of the Eurodollar markets. Banks in Europe would accept deposits denominated in dollars for clients that did not want to maintain such deposits in the United States. The banks in Europe would hold onto the deposits at the US banks, so the dollars never left the United States. This was a largely unregulated market that allowed depositors to earn higher returns than they would in the United States. Moreover, the Eurodollars were safe from confiscation by US authorities. The Eurodollar markets played a key role in the recycling of the deposits of oil-exporting nations in the 1970s as loans to oil importers, particularly in Latin America.

The end of the Bretton Woods regime came in 1973. The United States had suspended the convertibility of dollar assets for gold by foreign central banks in 1971. Central bank reserves had expanded during the US fiscal expansion due to increased spending on social programs at the same time as the war in Vietnam. European central banks, which feared the inflationary consequences of purchasing dollars in the foreign exchange markets, no longer wanted to be bound by the obligation to defend their countries' currencies against the dollar. Attempts to reform the system ceased two years later.

The Jamaica Agreements of 1976 allowed the IMF's members the ability to choose the exchange rate regime they thought appropriate for their countries. The United States, for example, gave up a fixed exchange rate in return for unregulated capital flows and monetary policy autonomy. Other countries, particularly developing economies, initially maintained capital controls to retain control of both the exchange rate and monetary policy.

The advanced economies, starting with the United States in 1974, opened their capital accounts after the end of the Bretton Woods regime. Much of the foreign investments that followed took place among this group of nations, unlike the capital flows from the United Kingdom to its former colonies in the earlier period of globalization. By 1980 almost two-thirds of world FDI was in Western Europe and North America (Jones 2005).

Developing countries did allow borrowings by their governments. The debt crisis of the 1980s arose when some of these nations, principally in Latin

America, were not able to make the payments on the bank loans they had taken in the Eurodollar market in the previous decade. The resolution of the crisis at the end of the decade through debt reduction and the exchange of loans for bonds contributed to the replacement of bank lending by portfolio flows.

Many emerging markets nations opened their capital accounts to some degree in the 1980s and 1990s. The IMF encouraged these countries to accept capital inflows to promote a more efficient allocation of global savings which would promote economic growth. In retrospect, there was little empirical evidence to support this position. Many East Asian countries engaged in deregulation, although the East Asian financial crisis of 1997–98 slowed this trend and brought a re-examination of the IMF's position.

Multinational firms played a key role in the expansion of global capital. They were often welcomed by domestic governments in developing countries because of their focus on exports. The firms also trained workers in modern technology and management methods. Over time, domestic suppliers of intermediate goods and other inputs would arise, and the benefits of the initial investment would expand. However, there could also be a rise in income inequality if foreign capital benefited workers with skills that could be used by the multinational firms but not less-skilled workers.

By 1990, therefore, changes were taking place that would lead to a global economy that rivaled the scope of the first era of globalization (Boughton 2012). First, political changes disrupted the isolation of former Communist countries. In Eastern Europe, the liberated countries sought to catch up with their more advanced neighbors. Economic liberalization in Russia led to soaring inflation and the takeover of state enterprises by a group of oligarchs. China began its reintegration into the world economy, which included FDI inflows, and rapidly became the dominant trading nation. Second, capital account deregulation allowed firms to expand across frontiers with the support of governments. In many cases these capital flows facilitated export-led growth, increasing trade linkages. Third, the advent of the World Wide Web and the development of personal computers allowed lenders and borrowers to keep in constant contact. Managers of multinational firms could supervise the activities of their subsidiaries around the world (Baldwin 2016).

Financial integration was checked by the global financial crisis of 2008–09. While central banks and the IMF moved swiftly to contain the disruption, the ensuing recovery was lethargic in many countries (Chen, Mrkaic, and Nabar 2019). FDI flows resumed but did not reach the same relative levels as before the crisis, in part due to governments' restrictions on foreign investments, particularly in the strategic sector. European banks reduced their international activities and were replaced in global banking in part by Chinese banks. Private and government debt, however, rose, fueled by the low interest rates enacted by central banks to facilitate the recovery.

The global economy suffered more shocks in 2020 as the COVID pandemic spread rapidly and in 2022 with the Russian invasion of Ukraine. The lack of resilience of global supply chains has led to a reconsideration of the advantages of foreign investments guided by low production costs. The resulting political fissures have set in motion a reconfiguration of the world economy, with trade and financial flows taking place within blocs centered on the United States, Europe, and Japan as one coalition and China, Russia, and Iran as a competing group (Section 8).

2.4 Summary

Foreign investment income is derived from the flows of capital that have arisen over time. Debt payments have been recorded since early civilizations flourished, while dividends were first paid by the European trading companies of the seventeenth century. Income flows grew during the first era of globalization, when unregulated capital flows were a key part of the international monetary trilemma adopted by governments. Foreign income was particularly important for Great Britain, the financial hegemon of the late nineteenth and early twentieth centuries.

Income flows collapsed during the First World War and the following interwar period, which saw the collapse of financial flows during the Great Depression. The Allied governments sought to avoid the chaos of that period through the Bretton Woods monetary regime, which allowed governments to use capital account regulations to maintain economic stability through monetary policy and fixed exchange rates. That consensus began to unravel in the 1950s as European banks held dollar deposits for their customers at US banks, which facilitated the recycling of oil revenues to oil importers during the 1970s. However, these loans could not be repaid and the countries that had borrowed experienced a lost decade in the 1980s.

The political openings of the 1990s were accompanied by waves of economic and financial deregulation. The advance of information and communications technology allowed multinational firms to establish and coordinate operations in developing economies with low production costs, and consequently FDI flowed to many of these countries. The profits made by the multinational companies contributed to the overall increase in the return on capital.

Bank activities expanded during the early 2000s, particularly as banks in the United States and Europe expanded their holdings of mortgage securities. The global financial crisis of 2007–09 ended their speculative activities and led to greater regulations and a contraction of the European bank sector. This was offset in part by an increase in the global activities of Chinese banks. The 2020 COVID pandemic and the Russian invasion of Ukraine were shocks that are reconfiguring the international financial system.

3 FDI Income: Receipts

3.1 FDI Income Surpluses

The earnings of a country's multinational firms appear in the primary income balance. As discussed in Section 1, net primary income includes the net flow of income received or paid for the provision of a factor of production, such as labor, financial, or other assets, to or from nonresidents. Investment income is usually the largest component of these income flows, and income from FDI is recorded as a component there with income from portfolio and other types of investments, as well as income from the central bank's reserves.

The amount of FDI related income reported by governments has risen over time as FDI flows across countries have increased. The Organization of Economic Co-operation and Development (OECD) reports the FDI receipts and payments for its thirty-eight members, which include the major recipient countries. Figure 3 shows the aggregate data for all members of the OECD from 2005 to 2022. The total net amount rose over time, with temporary declines in the wake of the global financial crisis and again during the global COVID pandemic, recovering to reach $603 billion in 2022.

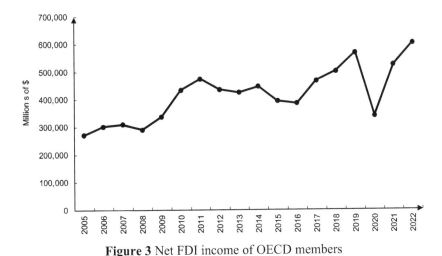

Figure 3 Net FDI income of OECD members

Source: OECD (2022)

Figure 4 shows the largest surpluses of FDI income in 2022. The receipt of FDI income is most concentrated among a few countries: the United States ($288,478 million), Japan ($174,177 million), the United Kingdom ($110,901 million), Germany ($99,575 million), and France ($80,943 million).

Figure 5 demonstrates that these advanced income countries have consistently received the bulk of foreign investment income flows over time (Gethin 2018). The United States has received approximately half of all the payments for much of the period. This predominance reflects several factors. First, FDI has historically been an important form of US international investments, and the United States owns a significant share of the stock of the world's stock of

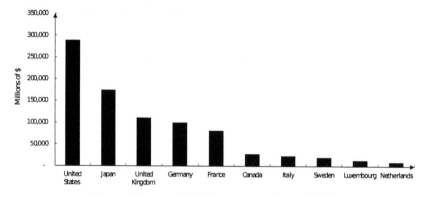

Figure 4 Largest FDI income surpluses (2022)

Source: IMF, *Balance of Payments Statistics*

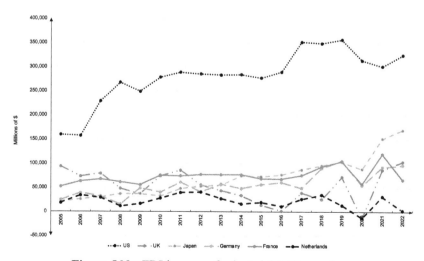

Figure 5 Net FDI income of selected OECD members

Source: OECD

outward investment (Lipsey 2003). In addition, the proportion of US firms reporting foreign earnings has risen over time (Dyreng and Hanlon 2021). Second, the return on US FDI assets has been higher than that paid on US FDI liabilities. This in part reflects the ability of US-based multinationals to take advantage of lower tax rates in foreign countries by shifting the source of their profits to these countries (see further). US firms may also be willing to undertake more risky projects abroad with higher payoffs.

Japan has become the second largest recipient of direct investment income. Rogoff and Tashiro (2015) claim that Japan earns higher than expected returns from maturity transformation. Fukuma, Morishita, and Nakamuta (2016) attribute the profitable returns to the growing share of direct investments in Japan's external assets.

The United Kingdom had been the second largest recipient of direct investment income for many years, but its earnings fell over the last decade before recovering in 2021 and 2022. Lane (2015) attributed the drop in earnings to decreases in the stock of the United Kingdom's direct investment assets as well as a decrease in the average yield on these assets relative to the liabilities. Langenmayr and Li (2023) found that multinationals based in the United Kingdom shifted profits to subsidiaries in low-tax countries after a change in the tax system.

Germany is also a major recipient of direct investment income. Knetsch and Nagengast (2017) present evidence that the increase in German investment income reflects the accumulation of foreign assets as well as changes in yields. Hünnekes et al. (2023), however, find that the returns on Germany's foreign assets, including FDI, are less than those recorded in other countries.

Unlike Japan and Germany, France has a negative net international investment position. However, in 2022 it had more FDI assets ($2.04 trillion) than liabilities ($1.50 trillion), which contributed to its surplus in FDI income. Vicard (2023) has also attributed the substantial gap between the returns on outward and inward investment to profit shifting by multinational firms based in France (see further).

3.2 FDI Income and Multinational Headquarters

The ranking of countries by their FDI income can be compared with the listing of countries by the number of multinational firms with headquarters located in their borders. Table 4 shows a ranking of countries by the number of Fortune Global 500 firms headquartered in their borders (Pizzola and Carroll 2024). The United States, Japan, Germany, and France appear at the top of the list. But the country at the number two position with the largest number of multinationals is China. Why does China not also appear in the list of top FDI recipients?

Table 4 Headquarters locations of Fortune Global 500
companies, 2023

Rank	Country	Number of Firms
1	United States	136
2	China	135
3	Japan	41
4	Germany	30
5	France	24
6	South Korea	18
7	United Kingdom	15
8	Canada	14
9	Switzerland	11
10	Netherlands	10

Source: Pizzola and Carroll (2024).

There are several reasons. First, China does not report the values of the components of its primary income, so its net FDI income is not known. But the Chinese government does report total net primary income, and that balance has almost always been negative. If FDI income is the largest component of primary income in China as it is for many other emerging market countries, then its net FDI income would also be registering deficits.

Second, while China is a net creditor nation with an overall net international investment position in 2022 of $2.4 trillion, its direct investment assets are less than its liabilities: $2.8 trillion vs $3.6 trillion, or net –$0.83 billion. While China has for many years been a major net recipient of FDI flows, these inflows have slowed sharply in recent years, reflecting concerns regarding the Chinese economy and geopolitical tensions. On the other hand, Chinese firms have expanded their activities in many developing economies, and these will increase its assets and income flow in the future.

Pizzola and Caroll (2024) point out that the headquarters of the multinational firms have over time shifted away from the United States and other members of the Group of 7 nations (Canada, France, Germany, Italy, Japan, and the United Kingdom). While the United States still accounts for the largest number of headquarters, the total number of firms with headquarters in the United States fell between 2000 and 2023. Japan also registered a decline in its multinational firms. The authors note a decline in the corporate tax rates in many other countries, which contributes to their appeal for firms willing to relocate. As other nations become the headquarters of multinational firms, their FDI income receipts will rise as well.

3.3 Tax Avoidance

Multinational firms usually pay income taxes in each of the jurisdictions where they have an affiliate that contributes to the firms' profits. The companies have used the differences in corporate tax rates across the host nations where the multinational's units operate to increase their overall profits. The practice, known as income shifting, results in higher earnings for the multinationals but less tax revenue for those governments with higher tax rates (Dyreng and Hanlon 2021).

In a global supply chain, different units contribute to the production of a final good. The host government can tax the value added to an imported intermediate input before it is sent to another host country where it will be further transformed into a final good ready for sale. Under a territorial tax system, the government of the home country where the firm has its headquarters only taxes the firm on its activities within its borders. Under a worldwide system, the government may tax all the income of its resident multinationals but allows the firms to claim credits for its payments of foreign taxes.

The tax each government can levy should be based on the market value of the transformed input minus its imported value. But if there is intra-firm trading, there is no market price for the intermediate good, and the firm assigns a value – the "transfer price" – that should approximate the market value. This practice gives the firms leeway in assigning values. In countries with high (low) corporate tax rates, the firm has an incentive to assign a higher (lower) value of the import and lower (higher) value of the export to decrease (increase) profits in that jurisdiction. The consolidated profits of the overall firm, therefore, will be higher.

Multinationals can also increase their profits in countries with low tax rates by assigning the ownership of intangible property, such as a trademark or other form of intangible property, to the affiliate based there. The firm's other affiliates pay fees to the unit in the low tax country for their use of the property, thereby lowering their profits and increasing those in the country with lower taxes. The company has the ability to assign ownership of the intangible property to any country it chooses.

Another method used by firms to increase total profits is the use of intra-firm lending. An affiliate of a multinational in a low-tax jurisdiction can lend money to another unit in a high tax country. The payment of interest on the loan can be deducted from the tax liabilities of the unit that received the loan to lower its tax liability, while the interest is taxed at a lower rate in the country which receives the interest.

The countries with low tax rates where profits are highest are "tax havens" or "offshore markets." Among the countries included in this group are Belgium,

Bermuda, Hong Kong, Ireland, Luxembourg, the Netherlands, Singapore, and Switzerland (Lane and Milesi-Ferretti 2018). There have been several attempts to estimate the size and extent of income shifting to tax havens. Tørsløv, Wier, and Zucman (2023), for example, estimated that about 36% of multinational profits in 2015, or $616 billion, was shifted to tax havens. Another study by Wier and Zucman (2022) found that the share of multinational profits shifted to tax havens rose sharply in the last decade before reaching 37% in 2019. They also observed that the share of multinational profits in global profits rose from 4% in 1975 to 18% in 2019, showing that the magnitude of the transfer has been increasing over time.

Another recent study by Garcia-Bernardo and Jansky (2021) reported that multinational enterprises shifted approximately $1 trillion of profits to tax havens in 2016, which resulted in an associated tax revenue loss of $200–$300 billion. Their results also indicate that low- and lower-middle-income countries tend to lose more tax revenue relative to their total tax revenue. They suggest that these countries should be represented on an equal basis in discussions of corporate tax reform.

3.4 Special Purpose Entities

Multinationals use special purpose entities (SPEs) to manage their income shifting and other activities. These are legal entities that allow foreign firms to use the host countries of the SPEs as conduits, with inflows of funds that pass through and are then routed to another country. The IMF (2020) has defined SPEs as:

> An SPE, resident in an economy, is a formally registered and/or incorporated legal entity recognized as an institutional unit, with no or little employment up to a maximum of five employees, no or little physical presence and no or little physical production in the host economy.
> SPEs are directly or indirectly controlled by nonresidents.
> SPEs are established to obtain specific advantages provided by the host jurisdiction with an objective to (i) grant its owner(s) access to capital markets or sophisticated financial services; and/or (ii) isolate owner(s) from financial risks; and/or (iii) reduce regulatory and tax burden; and/or (iv) safeguard confidentiality of their transactions and owner(s).
> SPEs transact almost entirely with nonresidents and a large part of their financial balance sheet typically consists of cross-border claims and liabilities.

These entities allow the multinational firms that use them to take advantage of lower tax rates and regulatory burdens, and to maintain the confidentiality of the income flows.

The top ten countries with a significant number of SPEs ordered by size of their inward FDI stock into SPEs are Luxembourg, the Netherlands, Hong Kong, British Virgin Islands, Switzerland, Singapore, Ireland, Cayman Islands, the United Kingdom, and Mauritius (Casella, Borga, and Wacker 2023). Their total FDI stock is estimated to be worth $11.7 trillion in 2016, and 70% of this aggregate, or $8.2 billion, is owned through SPEs. On a global basis, the stock of SPEs is estimated to be worth $12.3–12.5 trillion, which represents 36–37% of global FDI. The stock of capital available for productive uses, therefore, is overstated, and its actual allocation different from what official figures show.

The term "phantom FDI" has been used to refer to FDI that has no clear productive purpose, as opposed to "Real FDI" which does. Damgaard, Elkjaer, and Johannesen (2024) estimate that in 2017, phantom FDI of around $15 trillion represented almost 40% of all FDI and has been increasing over time. Luxembourg reported the largest amount of phantom FDI of $3.8 trillion, followed by the Netherlands with around $3.3 trillion. Hong Kong, Switzerland, Singapore, Ireland, Bermuda, the British Virgin Islands, and the Cayman Islands also hold a significant amount of phantom FDI. Hong Kong's holding of phantom FDI reflects its role as a financial conduit for Chinese firms.

SPEs pose a challenge to policymakers as they distort the size and direction of FDI flows and the income associated with them. The OECD has asked its members to report FDI-related data both with and without their SPEs. Not all the members have complied, but Luxembourg and the Netherlands have, and the differences between total FDI income and SPE-excluded income are striking.

Figure 6 shows Luxembourg's net FDI income between 2012 and 2021, the years when both data series are reported. Income with SPE income is much higher than the corresponding amount without SPE income. The difference was greatest in 2018 and has diminished since then. FDI income for the Netherlands shows a similar divergence.

3.5 Tax Agreements

Governments with multinational firms operating within their borders are aware of the loss of tax revenues due to multinational avoidance. Developing countries that rely on corporate tax revenues are particularly vulnerable to these practices. Many governments have lowered their corporate tax rates in part to provide an incentive for multinational firms to locate foreign investments in their countries. The result has been a "race to the bottom" as governments seek to establish an advantage over their competitors.

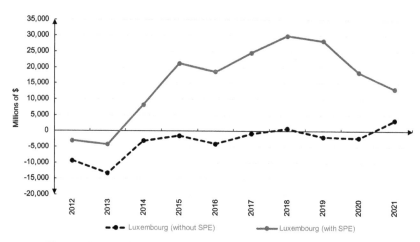

Figure 6 Luxembourg's net FDI income, with and without SPEs
Source: OECD (2024)

The OECD initiated the Base Erosion and Profit Shifting (BEPS) project in 2013 to organize a collective response by governments to multinational firms' use of the differences in countries' tax systems to lower their liabilities. In 2021, over 139 governments agreed to undertake a transformation of the global tax system. The structure, named the OECD/G20 Inclusive Framework of BEPS, would rest on two pillars.

Pillar 1 reallocates the right to levy taxes to include jurisdictions where sales of goods and services are made, including digital services. Its impact would be limited, as it would only affect multinational firms with revenues of more than $26 billion and profitability above 10% of revenues. Revenues would be linked to the market jurisdictions where the goods and services are used or consumed. Governments that agree to its provisions would refrain from taxing digital services separately.

Pillar 2 establishes a 15% Global Minimum Tax on multinationals through the Global anti-Base Erosion (GloBE) Rules. These include an income inclusion rule, which allows the government of a corporation's home country to treat all income as taxable, and to impose a "top up" tax on profits taxed at a lower rate elsewhere. There is also a provision that allows governments to tax intraunit payments that are made to affiliates located in low tax jurisdictions.

Much work has been undertaken on the details of the new tax provision. Estimates of the tax revenue gained by governments vary, but the OECD (2023) estimated at one point that Pillar 1 would yield $13–$36 billion and Pillar 2 $220 billion. However, the success of the accord depends on national governments agreeing to change their tax systems to conform with the provision of Pillars 1 and 2. US support, in particular, is seen as important to the overall success of the reforms.

3.6 Home Country Inequality

Past research has investigated the impact of FDI flows on income inequality (Eichengreen, Csonto, and El-Ganainy 2022), but FDI income has not been treated similarly. However, the earnings on FDI provide income, and its impact on income distribution can be studied for several reasons. FDI income surpluses, as shown earlier, are recorded for a small number of advanced economies. Within those countries, the upper-income segments of their populations benefit from the FDI income because of the concentration of stock ownership. In the United States, for example, the top 10% of stock owners hold 85% of all stock (Wolff 2021), and similar trends have been recorded for Europe (Zucman 2019).

Moreover, the compensation of corporate executives has been shown to respond to their firms' foreign activities. For example, Ma and Ruzic (2020) develop a model that shows that executives benefit more from increased profits in foreign markets than workers do and provide evidence that this channel is quantitatively important for the increase in top US income shares. Similarly, Keller and Olney (2021) found that foreign business activities increase the compensation of US top corporate executives, and this constitutes a channel whereby foreign income contributes to the income of those in the upper tiers of the distribution. Similarly, Kuwahata (2023) reported that outward FDI influences the compensation of Japanese executives. Joyce (2024) has shown that total FDI income reinforces the income share of the top 1% of households in the United States.

These results are consistent with the results of Carrera et al. (2024) that show a positive association between income inequality and external wealth. Those with larger shares of income accumulate external assets more than the general population. Financial globalization appears to have a significant impact on income inequality in the countries where the assets are held (Heimberger 2020).

3.7 Summary

The income generated by FDI has increased over time, although its growth was slowed by the global economic contraction resulting from the COVID pandemic. A significant proportion of this income stream flows to a few countries: the United States, Japan, the United Kingdom, Germany, France, and the Netherlands. The headquarters of the largest multinational firms are based in these countries, although an increasing number of multinationals have headquarters in emerging market nations.

The data on FDI income is distorted by the use of tax havens which offer corporations low tax rates. The multinationals can route their foreign activities to take advantage of the differences in taxation and record most of their profits in these countries. Many of the tax havens have SPEs that act as conduits for FDI capital flows from the originating nations to the ultimate recipients and for the resulting income flows in the opposite direction. The governments of the countries which have lost tax revenues as a result of this diversion have sought to reform the international system of taxation, and the OECD organized a series of conferences for its members that have devised regulations that would reallocate the profits of multinationals to the countries where the revenues are generated. The effectiveness of these proposals depends on whether they are enacted by national governments into their tax codes.

4 FDI Income: Payments

4.1 FDI Income Deficits

Matching the receipt of FDI income are the payments. There is a much wider distribution of countries with FDI income deficits than with surpluses. Figure 7 shows the countries with the largest net direct income deficits in 2022. These include Ireland ($140,667 million), Australia ($51,877 million), Brazil ($39,720 million), and Russia ($31,459 million). Ireland's position at the top of the list reflects its low corporate income rate that induces corporations to move there (Section 3). China most likely should be on this list, but its government does not report the components of investment income. On the other hand, Hong Kong, which serves as a financial conduit into China, does appear.

Many of the countries with relatively large FDI payments are emerging market nations (Joyce 2019). Net investment income registered deficits of 2–3% of GDP

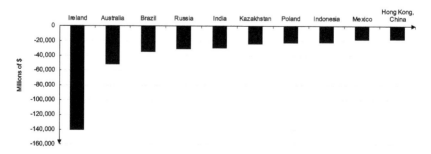

Figure 7 Largest FDI income deficits (2022)

Source: IMF, *Balance of Payments Statistics*

in a sample of twenty-six emerging markets over the period 1995–2015 (Joyce 2021). During this period, income payments on FDI liabilities came to surpass those on other types of foreign investment income (portfolio, other). In an empirical analysis of these payments, increases in the net stock of FDI scaled by GDP had positive effects on FDI payments. Moreover, capital account openness and trade openness also had negative and significant impacts. These results would be consistent with the governments of these countries deregulating their financial accounts in order to allow multinational firms to establish domestic affiliates. These affiliated firms subsequently engage in trade and generate income for their parent firms.

Advances in information and communications technology during this period allowed multinational firms to establish operations in countries with low production costs while maintaining control from their headquarters in their home countries (Baldwin 2016). The firms could arrange the production and shipment of intermediate goods in a large number of countries, with the partially finished good moving from country to country before its final assembly. The production of Apple's iPhone, for example, takes place in forty-three different countries, with its final assembly taking place in China (Ganapati and Wong 2023). Imports of intermediate goods account for significant proportions of world trade, and the value added to gross exports has been estimated to be about 70–75% (Johnson 2014).

This movement was facilitated by the easing of capital controls in many emerging market countries. The governments of these countries sought FDI for several reasons, including increases in exports, access to technology, foreign exchange that can be used for imports, and increased employment, often at higher wages. The use of widespread networks to integrate production processes also benefited from declines in transport costs. However, the experience of the COVID-19 pandemic demonstrated that supply chains can be significantly disrupted (Baldwin and Freeman 2021).

4.2 Impact on Current Account

The payment of income on FDI liabilities is seen by some as contributing to current account deficits and continued dependence on foreign capital in the host countries (De Beer and Rangasamy 2015; Yakubovskiy, Rodionova, and Derkach 2019). It could also be blamed for lower exports from the home country. However, the expansion of a multinational into a country need not result in a current account deficit in the home or host economies (Avdjiev et al., 2018).

Consider first the case of a multinational that produces and sends a good or service to the rest of the world (Table 5, Pre-FDI). Country A records a credit in its trade balance and its current account. These are matched by deficits in the balance of payments of the rest of the world.

If, however, country A's multinational establishes a subsidiary in Country B, the product will be exported from that economy, and a trade balance credit will be recorded (Table 5, Post-FDI). However, the profits from the sale belong to the parent unit. The payment is a debit entry in primary investment income for Country B that offsets the trade credit and leaves its current account undisturbed. Country A now has a surplus in its net primary income that leaves it with the current account surplus that the trade balance previously established. This transformation took place, for example, in Japan's balance of payments as its multinational firms expanded outside Japan. A country's current account balance, therefore, need not decline if its multinationals move their operations out of the country to another location.

Table 5 Income payments and current account

Pre-FDI

	Country A	Rest of World
Exports	50	0
Imports	0	50
X − M	+50	−50
Investment Income Receipts	0	0
Investment Income Payments	0	0
Net Investment Income	0	0
Current Account	+50	−50

Post-FDI

	Country A	Country B	Rest of World
Exports	0	50	0
Imports	0	0	50
X − M	0	+50	−50
Investment Income Receipts	50	0	0
Investment Income Payments	0	50	0
Net Investment Income	+50	−50	0
Current Account	+50	0	−50

Source: Avdjiev et al. (2018)

4.3 Retained Earnings

While the income generated by a multinational subsidiary in a host economy may be repatriated back to the home country, it may also be returned to the home country via the financial account in the form of retained earnings that contribute to new FDI (Table 6). Inflows of foreign direct investment can be financed through three sources of funds: new equity financing by a multinational, the reinvestment of earnings by the firm in the host country, or a loan from another unit of the multinational.

Total reinvested earnings have grown over time and are an important source of new capital flows (Strauss 2018). Figure 8 shows the components of global FDI financing from new equity, retained earnings, and debt (UNCTAD 2022). Retained earnings surpassed new equity in 2018, and since then the difference has grown in magnitude.

The decision over whether to finance new investment via a firm's retained earnings or through new financing has been analyzed in the finance and economics literature. The "pecking order of capital" hypothesis (Myers and Majluf 1984) claims that firms prefer to finance their expenditures through their own earnings first and then to utilize new equity raised from financial markets in order to retain control by the existing equity holders. Gertner, Scharfstein, and Stein (1994) compared retained earnings with bank lending and found several advantages for the former type of finance. The existence of earnings that can be used to finance foreign expansion can also be seen as a type of ownership advantage that multinationals possess in the framework of Dunning's (2001) eclectic paradigm of international production.

The literature on how multinational firms allocate their foreign earnings between repatriated dividends and retained earnings is limited. Several studies

Table 6 Financial Account

Current Account	Credits	Debits
Financial Account		
Direct Investment		
Equity		
Retained Earnings		
Equity Other than Reinvested Earnings		
Debt		
Portfolio		
Derivatives		
Other		
Reserve Assets		

Source: IMF (2013)

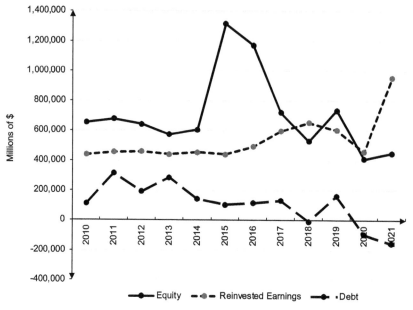

Figure 8 Financing of capital inflows

Source: UNCTAD

investigated the host country factors that have an impact on the retention of earnings. Oseghale and Nwachukwu (2010) found that the quality of domestic institutions as well as economic growth had significant impacts on the reinvestment of earnings by US multinationals. Chakravarty and Xiang (2011) examined the percentage of profits that were reinvested and reported that these were tied to access to external funding, the security of private ownership, and the extent of private ownership.

Polat (2017) investigated the determinants of the reinvested earnings, and his results indicated that they were affected by the level of GDP and its growth rate, and country risk as measured by the *International Country Risk Guide*. Zélity (2024), using bilateral country data, investigated the key determinants of FDI reinvestment rates. He found that geographical distance is inversely related to reinvestment, possibly because of agency problems, while a shared legal origin increases reinvestment. Higher world GDP growth reduces reinvestment, possibly because of better investment opportunities outside the host country.

4.4 Retained Earnings and Investment

There are many studies of the contribution of FDI on domestic investment through the acquisition of new capital and technology. If a multinational creates a subsidiary in the host nation with "greenfield FDI," this unit can use investment to obtain new capital goods. With "brownfield FDI," a multinational acquires or merges with an existing firm with its current equipment. The parent firm may subsequently decide to expand or update the existing capital stock. In addition, the entry of a foreign firm may encourage the creation of new domestic firms to provide inputs to the local unit of the subsidiary.

On the other hand, FDI may crowd out domestically financed expansion by raising the cost of investment or indirectly by forcing up the price of inputs. The funds may also be kept in liquid savings rather than new equipment. Amighini, McMillan, and Sanfilippo (2017) list thirty papers that present empirical evidence on inward FDI and new capital formation. In their own research these authors report evidence of a positive impact. However, the linkage depends on the type of activity undertaken by a foreign affiliate, as well as the technological distance between the home and host countries.

Several papers have investigated the impact of FDI financed by retained earnings on domestic investment. Ramirez (2011), for example, reported that FDI had a positive and highly significant impact on private capital formation in nine Latin American countries. However, the size of the coefficient was greatly reduced when the FDI variable was adjusted for the outward flow of profits.

Hansen and Wagner (2022) also examined the separate effects of retained earnings and non-retained earnings (new equity and debt) on gross fixed capital formation. They report significant coefficients for the lagged values of the former variable, while the latter has smaller coefficients with much less significance. When they aggregate both forms of FDI, the coefficient on FDI is similar in size and significance to those of non-retained earnings FDI, thus demonstrating the value of distinguishing between the two sources of FDI. They also find that inflows of retained earnings lower the probability of the occurrence of a financial crisis.

Other papers have investigated the impact on welfare due to FDI. Balcao Reis (2001) presents a model in which FDI lowers domestic welfare (i.e., the satisfaction of private and public needs), if foreign firms with better technology force out local, less productive producers out of business. Zélity (2022) presented a model calibrated with data from the Visegrád Four countries (Czech Republic, Hungary, Poland, and Slovakia). In this model increasing the number of foreign-owned firms enhances welfare due to the higher productivity of the local affiliates of the foreign firms. That enables them to pay higher wages and also lowers prices which raise the profit income of the households.

4.5 Volatility

FDI has generally been characterized as more stable than other types of foreign capital flows (Lipsey et al. 1999). The last few years, however, have been

Table 7 Standard deviations of sources of FDI finance, 1990–2020

	Equity	**Reinvested Earnings**	**Debt**
Advanced	1.21	0.30	0.88
Emerging Market	1.40	0.38	0.61

Source: IMF, *Balance of Payments Statistics*

marked by increased volatility in FDI flows. A steep decline in FDI flows occurred in 2020, but global FDI rebounded in 2021 (OECD 2022). This rise continued in the first quarter of 2022 but subsequently collapsed following Russia's invasion of Ukraine (OECD 2022). More generally, there has been evidence of an increase in FDI volatility (Broto, Diaz-Cassou, and Erce 2011; Pagliari and Hannan 2024).

If FDI flows have become more volatile, this should be reflected in the volatility of the different sources of FDI finance. An examination of the data confirms that the different sources of FDI flows vary in terms of their volatility. Table 7 shows the standard deviations of the three sources of FDI finance for two groups of countries, advanced and emerging markets (see Appendix for countries), averaged over the period 1990 to 2020. Equity financing has the highest standard deviation for both groups of countries, while retained earnings register the lowest standard deviation and the standard deviation of debt falls in between.

The stability of FDI flows and their impact on the host country's development may depend on how it is financed. The use of retained earnings to expand a multinational firm's existing operations may be seen as a "vote of confidence" in the economy. A government may seek to draw more reinvested earnings from multinationals already in its borders in order to have a more stable source of funding. Governments that assess FDI could examine the source of financing a particular inflow of FDI before admitting it. However, the research cited earlier has shown that global factors are responsible for at least part of the volatility of FDI as well as other forms of capital.

4.6 Summary

FDI income payments are recorded by countries that are host nations. In the emerging market countries, they are the result of FDI flows to these countries beginning in the 1990s as improved information and communication technology allowed multinationals to move operations from their home countries to foreign economies and coordinate the activities of all their subsidiaries. The offshore transfer of activities once undertaken in the home country may not worsen its current account as exports are replaced by direct investment income paid by the host economies of the foreign subsidiaries.

The decision over the use of retained earnings or new equity to finance a firm's operations depends on several factors, including the economic profile of the host country and the perception of political risk. Recent research has also sought to determine whether the retained funds are used for investment or for other uses. The evidence to date seems to indicate that retained funds are utilized to finance expenditures on capital goods and technology. This use may also reflect the lower volatility of retained earnings.

5 Portfolio Income

5.1 Equity and Debt Income

Portfolio flows include equity (stock) and debt (bonds) securities held outside the country of origin. The foreign owners of these securities receive dividends, interest, and capital gains. While evidence of debt agreements appears in the earliest records of civilization, tradeable bonds were first issued in medieval Italy (Section 2). Stock markets appeared later in the Netherlands and England.

Figure 9 shows the largest recipients of portfolio income. Like FDI income, the receipt of portfolio income is concentrated among a few nations: Japan ($79,102 million), Hong Kong ($33,655 million), Germany ($24,016 million), Norway ($16,371 million), and Kuwait ($14,740 million). Rogoff and Tahsiro (2015) claim that the return on Japan's portfolio debt assets is the source of the positive return differential between its foreign assets and liabilities. Norway and Kuwait are major exporters of oil and natural gas. Their foreign exchange

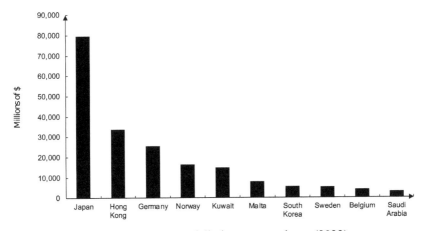

Figure 9 Largest portfolio income surpluses (2022)

Source: IMF, *Balance of Payments Statistics*

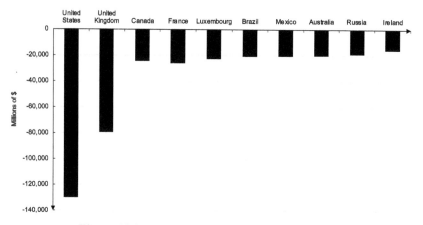

Figure 10 Largest portfolio income deficits (2022)

Source: IMF, *Balance of Payments Statistics*

earnings are held in their central banks as well as their sovereign wealth funds (Ajami and Karimi 2023).

The payment of portfolio income is more widely distributed, and Figure 10 shows the countries with the largest deficits in 2022. The major payers of portfolio income include the United States ($126,028 million), the United Kingdom ($79,139 million), Canada ($24,051 million), France ($23,186 million), and Luxembourg ($22,287 million). The United States, the United Kingdom, and France received FDI income while making payments on the securities that were issued by domestic firms and the government. In the case of the United States, this pattern has been attributed to the US role of "hedge fund to the world," borrowing by issuing debt to purchase real assets abroad. In addition, US Treasury bonds are considered to be "safe assets," despite the mounting debt of the federal government. A few other countries, such as Germany and Switzerland, also issue debt that is considered safe (Almadani et al. 2020).

Luxembourg, on the other hand, is an international financial intermediary. Its net outflows are based on the payments it receives from the securities held for investors in other countries (Sections 3.2, 3.4). Securities can be issued in a different country and registered there via a subsidiary established for that reason (Coppola et al. 2021; Florez-Orrego et al. 2023). When the lines of ownership are matched to the countries where the ultimate owners reside, then the geography of ownership of changes. Advanced economies, for example, have larger bond positions in emerging markets such as Brazil, China, and Russia than the conventional statistics indicate. Many of these bonds were issued in tax havens such as the British Virgin Islands, the Cayman Islands, Ireland, Luxembourg, and the Netherlands. In addition, Chinese equities are held more broadly than official statistics indicate, particularly by US investors.

The determinants of portfolio inflows can be divided into international "push" factors and domestic "push" factors. Empirical research on the drivers of stock and bond inflows finds consistent evidence that global risk aversion adversely affects portfolio capital flows to emerging market economies (Sarno, Tsiakas, and Ulloa 2016; Koepke 2019; Boonman 2023). Interest rates in advanced economies, and particularly the United States, also negatively impact these flows. Financial market development plays a positive role in attracting foreign capital. The resilience of these markets in advanced economies contributes to the greater importance of portfolio finance in those countries than in developing economies.

Portfolio flows have largely recovered from the effects of the global financial crisis. Portfolio bond flows to advanced economies continue to represent a significant proportion of their external debt flows. Bond financing by emerging markets has increased, which has offset a decline in bank lending (Committee on the Global Financial System 2021). Government-issued debt accounts for much of this borrowing.

5.2 FDI vs FPE

FDI and foreign portfolio equity (FPE) both involve some degree of ownership of a firm. Control of a domestic firm is assumed to exist when a foreign owner owns more than 10% of its equity. This control gives the foreign direct owners information about the domestic unit that foreign holders of stock do not possess, since they are dependent on the managers of a firm for information. The degree of control may be reduced if the FDI takes place through a merger with a domestic firm. On the other hand, liquidating real assets is more difficult than selling off stock. Potential investors, therefore, face a trade-off between efficiency and liquidity (Goldstein and Razin 2006). Developing economies are less like to possess liquid stock markets, however, and are less integrated with stock markets in the advanced economies (Kodongo and Ojah 2017). Consequently, they attract relatively more FDI.

Empirical analyses of the "pecking order" of foreign capital inflows have found that information frictions substantially reduce FDI flows (Daude and Fratzscher 2008). Other studies that have included distance as a friction also find that it lowers the flows of FDI relative to portfolio investment. On the other hand, portfolio investment is substantially more sensitive to the degree of financial market openness and development.

Portfolio investment's liquidity, however, can increase the chances of a "sudden stop," that is, an abrupt stop in capital inflows (Calvo 1998; Cavallo et al. 2015), and these can exert significant costs on the country.

A central bank with a fixed exchange rate loses foreign exchange reserves and may raise domestic interest rates to defend the exchange rate. The domestic private financial sector experiences a decline in the value of its assets while foreign depositors withdraw their funds. Private expenditures also fall, and all these reversals lead to a decline in real output.

FDI and FPE differ on one aspect of their respective measurements. Retained earnings are included in the calculation of FDI investment income and appear in both a country's current and financial accounts (Section 4). But retained earnings on FPE are not counted as investment income, and therefore do not appear in a country's balance of payments (Fischer et al. 2019). When the retained earnings on portfolio equity liabilities are measured and calculated, among the countries with the biggest adjustments to their balance of payments are the financial centers, such as Ireland, Hong Kong, Switzerland, and the Netherlands. Conversely, such payments are relatively small in emerging markets countries that do not receive portfolio equity inflows.

5.3 Diversification

Portfolio flows allow investors to take advantage of returns in other countries that may be higher than what they could earn domestically. Table 8 shows that on a global basis equity markets have returned an annual compounded nominal (real) return of 9.76% (5.80%) over the period 1960–2017 (Doeswijk, Lam, and Swinkels 2020). During the same period, private and government bonds provided average nominal (real) returns of 7.51% (3.63%) and 6.66% (2.81%), respectively. The returns on real estate are included for comparison.

The nominal equity return reflects a compounded capital gain of 6.64% and a dividend return of 2.92%, and standard deviations of 17.1% and 0.9%, respectively. Dividends do not have the same year-to-year fluctuations as

Table 8 Annual returns, 1960–2017

	Real Estate	Equities	Private Bonds	Government Bonds
Average Nominal Return (%)	10.45	9.76	7.51	6.66
Average Real Return (%)	6.46	5.80	3.63	2.81
Standard Deviation	19.30	17.30	8.40	7.33

Note: The average returns are compounded.
Source: Doeswijk, Lam, and Swinkels (2020)

stock markets exhibit. The dividend rate of return may have been influenced by the rise of corporate buybacks as a mechanism to return cash to investors.

The higher returns on stock and nongovernmental bonds come with more volatility. One way of lowering the risk on a portfolio of securities is to diversify the assets across different countries. It has long been recognized that a portfolio of assets from uncorrelated markets provides a way to attain a higher return with less risk than a strictly domestic portfolio could achieve.

However, investors do not take full advantage of this opportunity and hold a relatively higher proportion of domestic assets than finance theory indicates that they should. This phenomenon is known as "home equity bias," which reflects information frictions. There has been some evidence that home bias has decreased, in part due to increased globalization and regional integration (Baele, Pungulescu, and Ter Horst 2007).

Several studies have sought to determine whether the correlation of stock market returns across borders is increasing due to the increased impact of a global financial cycle. These studies find that the international diversification of stock holdings continues to provide benefits (Driessen and Laeven 2007; Coeurdacier and Guibaud 2011). The gains from portfolio diversification include mitigating market and political risks (Attig et al. 2023)

5.4 Risk Sharing

Foreign assets not only diversify a portfolio of assets but can also play a role in minimizing the fluctuations in domestic consumption that arise from idiosyncratic changes in the domestic economy. Foreign income flows can mitigate the drop in consumption that is due to a decline in the domestic economy. However, Lane (2001) reported that he had not found evidence of income smoothing with international investment income. Bracke and Schmitz (2011) tested whether income flows were countercyclical which could promote risk sharing, but could find any support for this linkage.

We can rewrite equation (1.6) to show the income from financial assets:

$$\text{GNI} = \text{GDP} + \text{A}^\text{D}\text{r}^\text{D} - \text{L}^\text{F}\text{r}^\text{F} \tag{10}$$

where A^D is the amount of foreign assets held by domestic residents and r^D is the return on these assets, L^F is the amount of domestic liabilities held by foreign residents, and r^F is their return.

If the return of the foreign assets is not correlated with domestic output, then asset returns can offset a drop in domestic income and smooth income. On the other hand, if the returns on domestic liabilities fall as GDP declines, then payments made by domestic firms to foreign creditors will also fall, which also contributes to income smoothing.

One way to test the degree of risk sharing would be to compare the change in domestic GNI minus the changes in foreign GNIs, that is, idiosyncratic GNI, on the difference between the change in domestic GDP minus foreign GDP, that is, idiosyncratic GDP.

$$\Delta \, logGNI_{it} - \Delta \, logGNI_t^F = \beta_0 + \beta_1 \, (\Delta \, logGDP_{it} - \Delta \, logGDP_t^F) \quad (11)$$

where GNI_{it} is GNI of country i in year t, GNI_t^F is aggregate foreign GNI in year t, GDP_{it} is GDP of country i in year t, and GDP_t^F, is aggregate foreign GDP in year t. The coefficient β_1 measures the co-movement between idiosyncratic growth in GNI with idiosyncratic growth in GDP. The lower the value of β_1, the more GNI is insulated from changes in the domestic economy. A value of unity for the coefficient would indicate no risk sharing through foreign-based income.

Researchers have sought to determine the degree of consumption smoothing by estimating:

$$\Delta \, logC_{it} - \Delta \, logC_t^F = \theta_0 + \theta_1 \, (\Delta \, logGDP_{it} - \Delta \, logGDP_t^F) \quad (12)$$

where C_{it} is consumption in country i in year t and C_t^F is foreign consumption in year t.

This coefficient θ_1 directly measures the relationship between idiosyncratic changes in domestic consumption and idiosyncratic output. A low value would indicate consumption can be protected to some degree from domestic accounts.

In early tests of the relationships, Sørensen et al. (2007) indicated that there was income risk sharing in the advanced economies. Kose, Prasad, and Terrones (2009) report that industrial countries attained better risk sharing outcomes during the period before the financial crisis. Developing countries, on the other hand, have not benefited. Similarly, emerging market economies, which received large increases in capital inflows, have seen little change in their ability to share risk. Islamaj and Kose (2022) test the impact of different types of capital flows on risk sharing in emerging markets and developing economies and find that capital inflows do not lead to better outcomes for sharing risk, while remittances and aid flows do.

Subsequent research has extended this framework in several ways (Balli, Basher, and Ozer-Balli 2011; Balli, Basher, and Ozer-Balli 2013). First, investment income was decomposed to income inflows versus outflows to determine which of these channels was dominant. Second, shocks to domestic GDP were split into positive and negative realizations to evaluate whether income smoothing operated in both cases. Finally, the empirical analysis was extended to include more countries and years.

5.5 Summary

Foreign financial assets provide income to the holders of the securities. The assignment of ownership of these assets is complicated by the use of foreign subsidiaries to register the security outside the home country. Uncovering the nationality of the ultimate issuers and owners of these assets reveals a different allocation than one based on tax havens.

While FDI and FPE represent a degree of foreign ownership of a firm, they differ in several important ways. FDI is sensitive to information frictions, while FPE investors are responsive to financial market development. The holders of FPE have more opportunities to diversify their portfolios. This diversification allows foreign investors to hold a portfolio with less risk than a purely domestic portfolio possesses.

Diversification can also diversify the sources of income and contribute to income smoothing. If changes in domestic income largely represent idiosyncratic factors, then foreign investment income can help the investors to smooth out their consumption. The empirical evidence shows that this form of risk sharing has been effective in advanced economies but not emerging market or developing economies.

6 Other Income

6.1 Other Income Flows

The category of other investment is defined by the IMF (2013) by what it does *not* include: "Other investment is a residual category that includes positions and transactions other than those included in direct investment, portfolio investment, financial derivatives and employee stock options, and reserve assets." This classification includes interest from bank deposits and loans, trade credit, and the use of IMF credit (IMF 2013).

Figure 11 shows the countries with the largest income surpluses in 2022. The major recipients of this form of investment income were Germany ($21,375 million) and Japan ($13,519 million), both countries with high savings rates.

Figure 12 shows the countries with the largest other income deficits in 2022. The largest net payers of this form of income were the United States ($29,517 million) and the United Kingdom ($18,787 million). These deficits were exacerbated by the increase in interest rates by their central banks in 2022 in response to higher inflation rates. Deficits were also recorded by India

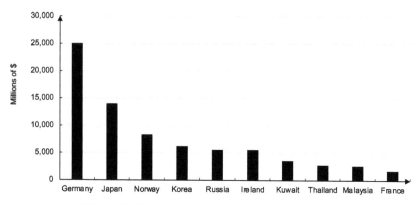

Figure 11 Largest other income surpluses (2022)

Source: IMF, *Balance of Payments Statistics*

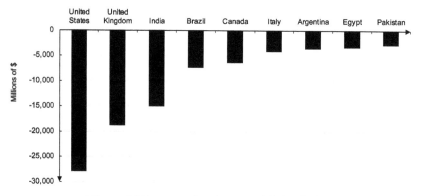

Figure 12 Largest other income deficits (2022)

Source: IMF, *Balance of Payments Statistics*

($15,044 million) and Brazil ($7,374 million). Both countries have public-owned banks that represent a significant share of banking activity.

6.2 Banking Activity

While evidence exists of banking-type lending occurring in early civilizations, the origin of modern banking is usually located in Renaissance Italy in cities such as Florence, Genova, and Venice (Kindleberger 1984). These family-controlled banks established a network through branches in other European countries. Banks were subsequently established in the Netherlands and Britain, and British hegemony in the nineteenth century was based in part on its status as an international banking center. Banks lent to sovereigns and commercial borrowers, and international lending became a major component of bank activity.

Banks function through the process of maturity transformation: they hold long-term assets and issue short-term liabilities. As long as withdrawals take place on a regular basis and can be matched with deposits backed up with adequate reserves, banks prosper by the spread between what they earn on the assets and what they pay on liabilities. Bank crises occur when a wave of withdrawals from bank accounts exhaust the amount of funds available to the bank to meet depositors' demands (Reinhart and Rogoff 2009, Ch. 10). These crises are exacerbated if there is a currency mismatch between its liabilities denominated in a foreign currency and its assets in the domestic currency.

Central banks and regulatory authorities can respond by making funds available to a bank, while the bank draws down its assets to redeem depositors' withdrawals. Such a response is appropriate when the crisis is a due to liquidity, that is, an inability to convert illiquid assets to cash. But when a bank's assets are less than their liabilities, the bank is insolvent and may need to be closed. If a wave of bank failures takes place, then the entire financial system can collapse.

Bank crises have taken place on a regular basis for centuries (Reinhart and Rogoff 2009). A banking crisis engulfed many European countries and the United States in the early 1930s and contributed to precipitating the Great Depression. Subsequent crises included the Asian Financial Crisis of 1997–98 and the Global Financial Crisis of 2008–09. These crises were preceded by a surge in credit fueled in part through international lending. In some cases, the inflows generated asset "bubbles" as the imported credit was used to buy domestic assets that rose in value before collapsing.

European banks were active participants in the US market for mortgage-based securities before 2008, and subsequently suffered large losses when that market failed. The initial crash in the US financial markets was accompanied or followed by collapses in the markets of several European countries. Similar lending had taken place in Ireland and Spain, while Greece had issued an excessive amount of sovereign debt.

European banks shrank their balance sheets in the wake of the crises, while changes in European bank regulation limited their expansion. Their place has been taken in part by Asian banks, but changes in capital requirements and other measures have kept international banking activity below its pre-crisis level. Rising interest rates increased profits in 2022 and 2023, but there were also bank collapses in the United States, including the Silicon Valley Bank and the First Republic Bank, while the Credit Suisse Group of Switzerland was acquired by the UBS Group.

6.3 Global Banking

International banking takes place in different arrangements. A bank headquartered in its home country can lend directly to a borrower in another country using the currency of either the bank or the borrower. In addition, a bank may obtain a third currency in an offshore market and make the loan in this currency (McCauley, McGuire, and Woolridge 2021). There are offshore markets in the dollar, the euro, the Japanese yen, and Chinese yuan. Exchange rate derivatives allow banks to hedge the foreign exchange risk of their lending activities. Banks can also establish subsidiaries in foreign countries to service clients there directly.

The impact of global banks on financial stability depends on several factors. Parent banks can support their affiliates during periods of instability, lessening the impact of local shocks. On the other hand, if the parent bank faces adverse conditions in its home country, borrowers in the host country may face withdrawals of funds. Studies of banking activity during the global crisis indicated that banks did transmit shocks across borders (Claessens and Van Horen 2013). In addition, borrowers who obtained credit in a foreign currency had to deal with exchange rate volatility that increased the value of their debt (Claessens 2017).

The determinants of the amount of credit extended to foreign borrowers have been widely studied. These studies usually differentiate between domestic and external conditions. For example, weak protection of property rights, legal inefficiency, and risk of expropriations have been found to be impediments to bank inflows (Papaioannou 2009). Other studies find that characteristics of the global banks, particularly bank size, are important determinants of the size of their foreign operations (Temesvary 2014). The balance sheets of the local subsidiary are also important, and lower capital to asset ratios and nonperforming loans at either the parent or affiliated bank reduced lending growth (Temesvary and Banai 2017).

Global factors have also been found to be important determinants of global bank lending activity (Shirota 2015). External funding costs, for example, have a large impact on global banks' lending (Aysun and Hepp 2016). Distance can affect international banking activities, which may be due to information frictions (Buch 2005).

The profitability of global banks has also been the subject of analysis, with home and host country characteristics under review. Foreign banks may be more profitable than domestic banks in a host country where the banking sector is less competitive, and where lower GDP growth rates and higher interest and inflation rates contribute to higher margins (Chen and Liao 2011). Bank profits have been found to be pro-cyclical, particularly during deep recessions (Bolt et al. 2012). Other studies of bank profitability have found that the results depend on the income level of the host country. Foreign banks underperform domestic banks in advanced economies, while the opposite seems to be true in emerging markets and developing economies (Claessens 2017).

There are also differences in the profitability of global banks in the advanced economies (Di Vito, Fuentes, and Leite 2023). European banks derive most of their profits from their lending activities, while US banks are more active in investment banking and trading activities. US banks have expanded their investment banking activities to Europe and other areas as European banks deal with the fallout from the global financial crisis. Consequently, European banks derive much of their revenues from interest income while the US banks rely more on fee and commission income as well as profits from trading activities.

6.4 Trade Credit

Trade credit is a form of short-term credit extended by a supplier to facilitate trade (Petersen and Rajan 1997). A supplier firm, for example, can offer a discount to an importing firm for early payment. A typical arrangement is "2–10 net 30," that is, a discount of 2% if payment is made within 10 days of the invoice, with full payment due within 30 days. Not receiving the discount can be seen as an interest charge for late payment (Wilner 2000). The credit is an account receivable for the supplier form and an account payable for the purchaser.

Trade credit can provide financing to a firm that may not be available from banks or other sources of finance (Petersen and Rajan 1997). Suppliers are able to fill the shortfall since they obtain information on their customers that they can use to evaluate their creditworthiness. The suppliers are also better equipped to seize the product and resell it in case of default by the customer. In some cases, the supplier can obtain bank credit that they channel to the purchasing firm.

Recent research has documented a decline in the use of trade credit since the early 2000s, particularly in the United States (Machokoto, Gyimah, and Ibrahim 2022). This decline has been linked in part to the institutional development of financial markets and institutions in developed economies, as firms rely less on trade credit when access to bank credit improves. Firms in emerging markets economies without an extensive banking system, however, continue to depend on trade credit. In these cases, firms that use trade credit may grow more quickly than firms that do not (Fisman and Love 2003). A decline in the supply of trade credit in these countries would particularly affect smaller and newly established firms that do not yet qualify for bank credit.

Wilner (2000) has presented a model of trade credit's interest rate. In this work, dependence in lending relationships affects the pricing of contracts. A dependent creditor grants more concessions in negotiations over the terms of the credit than a creditor without such a relationship. However, the creditor will charge a higher interest rate to compensate for the concessions. In an empirical analysis, Klapper, Laeven, and Rajan (2012) found that riskier buyers are offered discounts to repay earlier which allows the supplier to contain the credit risk in their portfolio.

6.5 Summary

The net other income balance includes several forms of income, and bank income is the largest component for most countries. Banks earn profits from the spread between the interest they receive from their assets, usually loans, and what they pay on deposits. Banks usually possess sufficient liquid assets available to handle redemptions by depositors, but occasionally they face a liquidity crisis when there is a large-scale wave of withdrawals. If not corrected, the liquidity crisis can become a bank crisis where banks are insolvent.

Global banking includes the activities of banks that take place on an international scale, either through the parent unit lending to a foreign borrower or extending credit via a foreign subsidiary established for that purpose. There are also offshore markets that allow banks to lend to borrowers in foreign currencies and are often loosely regulated. Global banks can lend to a subsidiary when the conditions in the host country deteriorate. But the global banks can also withdraw funds from their foreign units when the host country faces financial and economic shocks.

Studies of the amounts of credit extended to foreign borrowers find that they reflect domestic conditions, such as the status of property rights, and characteristics of the banks themselves, such as their size. Bank profitability depends, in part, on whether the host country's economy is advanced or emerging. There are also differences between the activities of European banks and those of US banks.

Trade credit income is also included in this component of international income. Trade credit is a form of short-term credit extended by a supplier firm to a customer. Firms in developing economies without extensive banking systems can use trade credit to manage their payments.

7 Transfer Payments

7.1 Secondary Income

In addition to primary income, the current account also includes net secondary income. Like primary income, secondary income has risen over time.

This section offers an analysis of secondary income as a contrast to the previous sections.

Secondary income includes transfers, which are payments without a corresponding exchange. These payments between residents and nonresidents can be made by individuals, governments, or international organizations. They are included in Gross National Disposable Income (Section 1).

Personal transfers are usually made by laborers who leave their home country in search of better positions with higher wages. When they are successful, they often send money to their home country in the form of transfers. These payments offer an interesting comparison to investment income flows in their origins, history, size, and impact.

Figure 13 shows the countries with the largest net secondary income surpluses in 2022. In absolute terms, India ($97,319 million) and Mexico ($58,077 million) have the largest surpluses, which reflect the large amounts of personal transfers made to their residents. Figure 14 displays the countries with the largest secondary income deficits. These are mainly countries that host many immigrants, such as the United States ($168,959) and Germany ($72, 456 million).

There is a distinction between transfers and remittances. The IMF and the World Bank base their measures of remittances on two sources that appear in different components of the current account. The first is the net income of residents employed by foreign firms and governments, including the wages paid to temporary migrant workers in other countries. These data are recorded in the primary income account. The second component consists of the personal transfers made or received by residents, and these are reported in the net secondary income account. Transfers are usually much larger than the income earned from foreign firms or governments. Chami et al. (2008) have cautioned

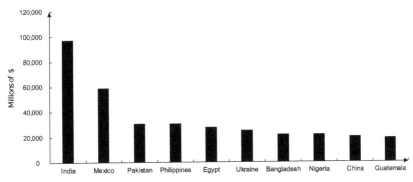

Figure 13 Largest secondary income surpluses

Source: IMF, *Balance of Payments Statistics*

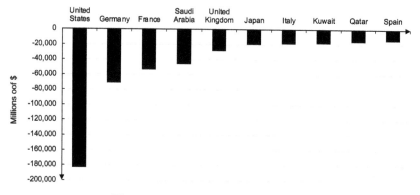

Figure 14 Largest secondary deficits

Source: IMF, *Balance of Payments Statistics*

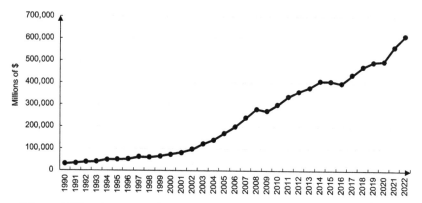

Figure 15 Remittances to low- and middle-income countries, 1990–2022

Source: World Bank, *World Development Indicators*

that these two types of payments may have different relationships with macroeconomic variables of interest, such as GDP per capita.

Total remittances are estimated to have totaled $790,875 million in 2022, according to the World Bank. Most of these funds ($614,343 million) were directed to low- and middle-income countries. Figure 15 shows the rise in these remittances since 1990.

The top recipient countries in 2022 were India ($111 billion), Mexico ($61 billion), China ($51 billion), the Philippines ($38 billion), and Pakistan ($30 billion) (Ratha et al. 2023). When ranked by remittances as shares of GDP, the top recipients were Tajikistan (51%), Tonga (44%), Lebanon (35%), Samoa (34%), and the Kyrgyz Republic (31%). The United States is the largest source of remittances when measured in dollars, while Saudi Arabia is second in dollar terms and largest when remittances are scaled by GDP.

However, all these data are limited by the use of informal channels to send money because these payments are often unrecorded (see further). These flows hinder the attempt to collect accurate data and can be subject to theft or diverted to illegal uses. As a result, the governments of the recipient countries and international organizations, including the IMF and the World Bank, are cooperating to formulate new methods to widen their measurements of remittances.

7.2 History of Migration Flows and Remittances

Migration flows of the modern era have often mirrored international capital flows (Solimano and Watts 2005). Just as capital flows increased during the first era of globalization, so did the migration of people. The countries of the Americas as well as Australia and New Zealand attracted both capital and labor from Europe. The natural resources of the new countries yielded higher wages and rates of return than were available at home. The flow of migrants was facilitated by improvements in the technologies of transport and communication financed by capital inflows, which lowered the costs and uncertainty of migration (Hatton and Williamson 2008).

The number of Europeans who came to the Americas and Australia during the 100 years between 1820 and 1920 has been estimated to be 60 million. Migrants initially came primarily from Great Britain and Germany. They were followed by people from other areas, including the Scandinavian countries, Southern Europe, and Eastern Europe. Many journeyed to the United States and Canada, but there were also substantial flows to Argentina, Brazil, and Mexico as well as Australasia. Ethnic discrimination against Chinese immigrants in the destination countries, however, became institutionalized through quotas and other administrative procedures.

The mass migrations of the nineteenth century were followed by flows of income to the migrants' home countries. Many of these migrants were young men who sought to support family members at home. Sometimes they were followed by other members of the extended family who could afford the cost of travel because of the remittances.

These migrants used different channels to send money to their home countries. Family friends making the trip home were entrusted with carrying cash, while currency was sent by mail. As the remittances increased in value, formal channels grew in importance. These included money orders, money transfers via the Western Union Corporation, and the use of banks with branches in both the host and home countries.

The means to send money across borders existed for Chinese and Indian migrants as well. Chinese migrants would send money home via labor recruiters who also functioned as couriers. Private postal exchanges were also established to facilitate the transfer of funds for Chinese migrants (Lim 2019; Shiroyama 2019). Indian migrants who sent money home would often use the hawala system, which consists of a system of brokers who would collect and disburse funds (Afram 2012).

The use of informal means to send money home limits the availability of data, and studies by economic historians have sought to extrapolate from the existing data the total amounts of funds that were sent. One study (Esteves and Khoudor-Castéras 2009) used studies for individual countries to estimate remittances as shares of GDP for six European countries between 1880 and 1913. On average over this period Italy recorded the highest levels of remittances when scaled by GDP, 2.8%, which was followed by Portugal (2.7%), Spain (1.2%), Austria-Hungary and Sweden (both 0.8%), and the United Kingdom (0.4%). These payments followed a countercyclical pattern, rising when the home country's economy contracted and the migrants increased their payments to aid their families.

Migration from Europe, which had been falling as European wages rose during the early twentieth century, collapsed during World War I as borders closed, matching the shutdown of capital flows. The numbers of migrants began to rise during the postwar era, but never resumed the levels attained during the prewar era. The United States, the principal destination country, imposed restrictions on the numbers of people admitted from Southern and Eastern Europe, as well as on Asian countries. Other destination countries also passed legislation to regulate the flows of people. The worldwide economic contraction of the 1930s hampered the search for jobs, while the outbreak of World War II once again closed national borders.

The end of World War II and the subsequent worldwide economic recovery led to the resumption of migration. However, governments continued to monitor and regulate the flows of people across their frontiers, and migration never returned to the same relative magnitude as it had before 1914. Similarly, capital controls, which were permitted by the 1944 Bretton Woods agreement, restricted capital flows.

But migration rose during the 1970s, which is also the period when capital flows among the advanced economies began to increase. The fall of the Soviet Union and the removal of restrictions on travel in Europe led to a further rise in migration in the 1990s, including within Europe. The foreign-born share of the population in Oceania increased about one third between 1965 and 2000, more than doubled in North America, and more than tripled in Europe (Hatton and Williamson 2008). These changes reflect in part the end of selective policies that assigned quotas by national origin and curbed migration from Asia.

Hatton and Williamson (2008) have identified significant differences between the migration of the first era of globalization and its post–World War II counterpart. First, Europe switched from an emigration source to a destination for migrants. It attracted people from Asia, the Middle East, and Africa, while migrants from Eastern Europe traveled to Western European nations. Second, Latin America was transformed from a migration destination to a source of migrants, particularly to North America. Third, the numbers of Asian and African migrants grew significantly. Fourth, the development of oil production in the Persian Gulf area led to a demand for laborers, particularly in construction and domestic services. While many workers came from other Arab countries, there were also large numbers of Asian workers. Finally, there was an enormous increase of workers from East European nations no longer under the control of the Soviet Union to the West European countries.

The number of migrants rose in the twenty-first century from 173 million in 2000 to 281 million in 2020 (United Nations 2020). As a share of the world population, the share of migrants in the world population stock increased from 2.8% to 3.6% (EMM 2.0). The amounts of remittances matched the rise in migrant flows, from $126 billion in 2000 to $702 billion in 2020. The payments fell slightly during the pandemic but rebounded in the following years. However, it is important to keep in mind the inexactitude of these data. Remittances continue to be sent through formal and informal channels. The reported rises may indicate increases in the amounts of remittances that are now reported that were not known before.

The determinants of the choice of the amount of remittances and their transmission can be studied using either an "altruistic" or the "investment" approach, also known as "self-interest" (Carling 2008; Yang 2011). In the altruistic-based analysis, migrants send money home to improve the welfare of their families. The investment approach posits a transfer of funds home by the emigrants to the families who manage investments for the migrant. The two approaches need not be exclusionary.

Empirical analyses have shown that several key factors determine the amounts of remittances. These include the costs of sending the funds, the state of financial development in the home country, and the level of education of the migrants (Kosse and Vermuelen 2014). A study comparing workers remittances with capital flows to developing countries shows that the remittances respond more to demographic variables, while capital flows respond to macroeconomic conditions (Buch and Kuckulenz 2009).

In addition, the cost of the transfer also influences the choice of channel (Freund and Spatafora 2008). The costs of sending remittances have been estimated at 6.2% for a payment of $200, but this is an average figure. Banks continue to be the costliest channel for sending remittances, with an average cost of 12% (Ratha et al. 2023). The cost for digital remittances is lower than the cost of nondigital remittances, and the progress of financial technology may bring costs down further. The United Nations has selected the reduction of the costs of sending remittances to 3% as one of its Sustainable Development Goals. In 2020 the Group of 20 nations made the enhancement of cross-border payments a priority, and its members now submit National Remittances Plans which report measures undertaken to facilitate the transfer of funds across borders.

7.3 Impact of Remittances

Remittance payments to developing economies are the largest source of foreign income for many of them, surpassing FDI inflows or official aid. The impact of remittances has been widely studied. Among the positive impacts found on the micro level are increases in the consumption of the households that receive them, better access to education and healthcare, and improved creditworthiness (Amuedo-Dorantes and Pozo 2023).

The macroeconomic impacts of remittance flows have also been examined (Chami et al. 2008; De et al. 2019; Cazachevici, Havranek, and Horvath 2020). Remittances can raise economic growth if there is an increase in investment domestically or a rise in total factor productivity due, for example, to higher spending on education. Growth could also be boosted if there is a positive effect on the country's financial system resulting from increased financial flows. On the other hand, remittances can deter growth through an appreciation of the exchange rate that leaves exporters at a disadvantage, a phenomenon known as the "Dutch disease." In addition, the recipients of the funds may reduce their supply of labor and make risky investments.

Remittances can also affect macroeconomic volatility. Migrants increase their transfer payments in response to a downturn in their home country, which allows the recipients to smooth consumption (Kose, Prasad, and Terrones 2009). In addition, remittances may bolster domestic financial institutions and markets, which provide funds for less volatile investment. Empirical studies have generally found that remittances flows do dampen domestic economic volatility. Moreover, remittances themselves may be less volatile than other external resources.

Remittances may reduce the likelihood of financial crises that impact the current account (De et al. 2019). The stable inflow of foreign exchange which remittances provide can reassure investors who are concerned about a sudden reversal of capital flows (Bugameli and Paterno 2009). The funds also allow higher levels of government expenditures and public debt. Remittances have a positive impact on the credit ratings of sovereign debt (Chami et al. 2008), consistent with these transmission mechanisms between remittances and greater financial stability.

There are also studies of the relationship of remittances and the current account. There is a positive accounting relationship as a rise in remittances increases the credit entries in the current account. However, there may also be negative effects, depending on whether the funds are saved or spent, and if the latter, on domestic goods or imports (Hassan and Holmes 2016). In addition, as pointed earlier, the remittances may lead to a real exchange rate appreciation (Acosta, Lartey, and Mandelman 2009; Lartey, Mandelman, and Acosta 2012). Hasan and Holmes (2016) find that remittances can facilitate a sustainable current account, particularly in countries with high remittance flows. Lartey (2019) finds that remittances have a positive contemporaneous effect on the current account, but a lagged negative effect which he ascribes to the Dutch disease phenomenon. A more flexible exchange rate dampens the positive contemporaneous impact.

An investigation of current accounts and their secondary income components reveals several cases where the magnitude of remittances is significant with respect to the trade balance. Mexico, for example, registered a 2022 current account deficit of $18,046 million. Its trade deficit of $42,292 million was much larger, as was the primary income deficit of $33,831. But the secondary income balance showed a surplus of $58,077 million, reflecting the personal transfers of Mexican workers, which partially offset the effect of the trade and primary income balances. Mexico's situation is not unique; Egypt, for example, has a similar configuration in its current account.

7.4 Capital and Labor

The flows across borders of capital and labor can play important roles in making the world economy more efficient (Siebert 2002). Capital is directed to those economies that offer the highest promise of return, while workers leave their native lands in search of higher wages. Investment income and personal transfers reflect the subsequent returns to these productive factors.

In the classical trade model of Heckscher-Ohlin, the factors of production are substitutes and internationally immobile. Countries that are capital-abundant export those goods that are capital-intensive in their production, while labor-abundant economies produce labor-intensive goods. Changes in the prices of goods due to trade flows lead to the equalization of factor prices across frontiers. Mundell (1957) showed that in the absence of international trade, factor flows would accomplish the same end.

Many empirical studies have sought to measure the elasticity between capital and labor (Gechert et al. 2022). There have been episodes in the global economy, however, where the international movements of capital and labor were complementary. Clarke (1995), for example, points out that in the pre–World War I period both factors flowed from Great Britain to the United States and other countries which were abundant in natural resources.

Research on capital flows and migration in the most recent period has supported the premise that capital flows and migration can follow each other. Migration, for example, can facilitate bank loans to the home countries when it reduces informational frictions (Kugler, Levintal, and Rapoport 2018). A similar linkage has been found in the case of FDI and migration (Kugler and Rapoport 2007). This effect is particularly strong when the migrants are skilled laborers (Gheasi, Nijkamp, and Rietveld 2011). On the other hand, inward FDI could encourage emigration from the host country by making travel more feasible (Bang and MacDermott 2019). Sanderson and Kentor (2008) offer evidence that FDI to developing economies increase emigration from these countries. These different linkages can coexist and reinforce each other.

Regardless of the nature of the international linkages between capital and labor, the geographical record of their associated income flows demonstrates their origins in the relative factor abundance of their source countries. Investment income primarily flows from emerging markets that have become capital importers, such as China, Brazil, and India to the countries that are capital-abundant and own the assets that generate the investment income, particularly Japan, Germany, the United States, and France. The capital flows from these countries are net flows. The United States is the world's largest recipient of FDI, while China is the home country of many multinationals that invest outside its borders. Remittances flow from countries which host laborers, such as the United States and Saudi Arabia, to those countries with an abundance of labor, which include many developing economies.

A country's relative factor flows can change over time. The patterns of labor migration have changed over time, and in the most recent period, Asia has been a major source of international migrants. The aging of work forces in Asia and Europe and the response of laborers to new opportunities will lead to further configurations of remittances flows.

7.5 Summary

Transfers are a form of income that flows across borders. Most of the payments are made by migrants from developing economies who reside and work in another country. These payments have risen over time, although this increase may reflect better recording by government authorities. Several factors affect the amount of remittances, including the cost of transmission. Lowering the cost of sending funds across borders has become a policy goal for several intergovernmental organizations.

The impact of remittances on the recipient country has been widely studied. Many of these studies have investigated the effect on consumption, education, and healthcare. There are also macroeconomic outcomes, such as lower volatility due to increases in payments sent in response to economic downturns in the home country. The immediate effect on the current account of a payment is positive, but there can be negative follow-up consequences if imports rise or if there is an appreciation of the domestic currency.

The migration of people searching for work matched capital flows in the nineteenth century as the emerging markets of that era (United States, Australia) attracted both laborers and investments. In the twentieth century, relative factor endowments changed, as did the flows of productive resources. The large amounts of remittances received by developing countries reflect their relative abundance of people. Further migration in response to dwindling labor forces in Europe and Asia will lead to new flows of remittances.

8 Future of Investment Income

8.1 Fragmentation

The future of international capital flows and the resulting income generated by them has become blurred by the geopolitical and economic events of the last fifteen years. The global financial crisis, the election of Donald Trump who imposed tariffs on Chinese and other countries' products, and the withdrawal of the United Kingdom from the European Union led to a slowdown in the growth of capital flows. The COVID pandemic demonstrated the fragility of global supply chains, while the Russian invasion of Ukraine deepened the fissures among countries.

Global FDI flows fell by 7% in 2023, continuing a downward trend following the pandemic (OECD 2024). FDI inflows to the Group of 20 countries fell by 34%, and by 46% to the non-OECD members of the Group of 20. Despite a drop in 2023, the United States remained the largest recipient of FDI inflows ($341 billion), followed by Brazil ($64 billion) and Canada ($50 billion). China's FDI inflows continued a long-run decline, from $190 billion to $43 billion. Net FDI income for the OECD members in 2023 was virtually the same as in 2022, $613 billion.

The IMF reported a steep drop in global FDI flows from 3.3% of GDP in the 2000s to 1.3% between 2018 and 2022 (IMF 2023). The IMF's 2023 flagship

World Economic Outlook examined the changes in the allocation of FDI in recent years and their impact. The authors noted that trade and capital flows have fragmented along geopolitical lines. If this new pattern continues ("friend-shoring"), FDI will become more concentrated within blocs of politically aligned countries. Other forms of capital flows, such as portfolio flows, are not immune to this reallocation.

This relocation of multinational activities will have negative effects on emerging markets and developing economies that are not politically aligned with the United States or China. These countries depend on FDI for capital and technological deepening, and their own companies benefit from the competition with foreign firms. Reductions in FDI related to vertical integration, which is associated with economic growth, are particularly costly for these countries.

The IMF's authors also looked at FDI flows that included "strategic FDI," that is, FDI linked to national and economic security concerns. The flows of strategic FDI to Asian countries, and particularly China, have fallen sharply. On the other hand, this type of FDI was more resilient in Europe and the United States. The allocations point to a growing gap between Europe and Asia in this sector.

The issue of fragmentation also appeared in an IMF paper by Gopinath et al. (2024). The authors take note of the reallocation of trade and investment flows among countries, triggered in part by the tensions between the United States and China. Trade flows and FDI between a US-centered bloc and a China-centered bloc have declined by 12–20%, more than trade and investment within countries in the same bloc. However, several countries, such as Mexico, Canada, and Vietnam, serve as connectors, receiving Chinese goods and reexporting them to the United States.

A similar assessment of the changes in global trade and investment is offered by Eichengreen (2024). Investments that might have gone from the United States to China and vice versa now are directed to third countries that serve as bridges between the two. This (supposedly) leads to an improvement in national security in exchange for less efficiency. But it may take years to form a quantitative assessment of that trade-off.

Many of these themes also appeared in a UNCTAD (2024) report, *Global Economic Fracturing and Shifting Investment Patterns*. These authors also find evidence of fracturing in global FDI along geopolitical lines and evidence of instability in investment relationships. They point to a gap between investment in the manufacturing and services sectors, with the latter growing in importance. The slowdown in manufacturing hinders the ability of smaller economies to participate in global production.

8.2 Industrial Policy

As part of their response to perceived external threats, many governments are instituting industrial policies. These policies are designed to achieve self-sufficiency in key sectors, such as the technology used for national defense or for clean energy. They include subsidies, low-cost loans, and the use of trade barriers to deter foreign competitors. China has long promoted its industrial development, particularly in manufacturing, to raise economic growth through exports. More recently the Chinese government has sought to promote the domestic development of advanced technologies to reduce the country's dependence on foreign suppliers.

In the United States, the Biden administration built upon tariffs imposed by President Trump to bolster the domestic production of technology related to security concerns, such as the production of computer chips. It also subsidized investments in the transition to clean energy. The European Union has developed its own industrial policy to promote high-tech industry and green technologies. There are areas of overlap with the US plans and those of the European Union, and the two sides have sought to minimize friction and promote partnership whenever possible.

8.3 New Financial Centers

International financial centers link lenders and borrowers on a global basis, providing a range of financial services. These include not only banks but also law firms, accountants, insurance brokers and other service firms that facilitate capital flows. For many years this role was served mainly by firms in London and New York. But the emerging market economies have their own financial centers, and increasingly serve clients in their regions. These cities include Singapore in East Asia, Mumbai in India, and Dubai in the Gulf states. There are also offshore financial centers which primarily serve to assist corporations and wealthy individuals lower their taxes. Jersey and the Cayman Islands are examples of such jurisdictions.

The regional centers provide several advantages over the traditional financial hubs (Hatayama 2019). First, they may be able to insulate their regions from instability in the advanced economies. Second, they have sources of knowledge about local investment opportunities that they can finance. Third, they facilitate FDI and private equity inflows. Fourth, they promote investments among emerging markets and developing economies, making them less dependent on the advanced economies. Fifth, these centers can play an important role in financing the transition to sustainable energy.

8.4 Fintech

The future of international capital and investment income will be shaped not only by government policies and regulations but also by the use of financial technology ("fintech"). Private fintech firms use digital technology to provide financial services that are cheaper and more accessible than those provided by the traditional financial firms. These include cross-border payments, including remittances, and facilitating the sale of private crypto assets. Central banks are considering the use of issuing digital currencies (CBDCs), and the implications for banks and other financial institutions of such an innovation are under study (Banerjee 2020).

The impact of fintech on capital flows is also under investigation. Initial results indicate that a country with a higher level of digital financial development is more likely to experience capital inflow surges (Gou, Li, and Zhao 2024). The mechanisms that lead to the increase include the convenience of this technology in providing access and payments. Fintech may also contribute to financial contagion through the rapid dissemination of changes in investors' asset evaluations.

Governments are aware of the benefits and costs of financial technology. The IMF and the World Bank Group organized the Bali Fintech Agenda in 2018 to provide policymakers with the opportunity to adapt existing regulatory tools and develop new ones that will ensure that this new technology is beneficial for all. A twelve-point Agenda provided a framework for the discussion (IMF 2018), which acknowledged that fintech could provide financial services to those who have been underserved by existing financial institutions and markets. The Agenda also urged the modernization of legal frameworks to provide clear rules to guide the development of new technologies, while ensuring the stability of domestic monetary and financial systems. In addition, the Agenda called for international cooperation and information-sharing among policymakers to ensure effective policy responses. This included roles for the IMF and the World Bank in improving collective surveillance procedures to manage the balance of risks for global financial stability.

8.5 Future Developments

The fragmentation of the global economy affects the allocation of capital. Government policies are establishing barriers between blocs of countries, and as a result capital flows no longer are directed to the areas with the best risk-reward features. This new distribution will slow down economic growth and the income generated by the efficient allocation of capital.

But there are forces operating in the opposite direction. First, emerging market and developing economies channel capital to each other (Hufbauer and Adler 2010; Sengupta and Noeth 2012; Schroth 2023). Outward FDI by Chinese multinational firms rose from \$43,890 million in 2009 to \$149,692 million in 2022, and a significant amount of the recent outflows was directed to other developing economies (*The Economist* 2024). If trade restrictions block the sales of Chinese products to many of the advanced economies, then these other markets provide an alternative for Chinese commercial expansion. Second, fintech firms are providing financial services and products that can expedite the movement of funds, such as making payments and cross-border lending, around the world. Remittances have also been expedited. Third, private firms will seek to establish new sources of income in markets where they may not have operated before.

8.6 Summary

Economic and political shocks, such as the global financial crisis and the COVID pandemic, have contributed to a fragmentation of the global economy, and over time developing economies may suffer most keenly the economic repercussions. While there are still extensive cross-border trade and financial linkages, more economic transactions are taking place within rival blocs. Many governments base their capital flow regulations on their industrial policies designed to shore up strategic sectors.

There are some counter-developments. New financial centers provide alternative sources of finance between emerging markets and developing economies. The governments of countries not closely aligned with either geopolitical bloc seek to maintain commercial and financial ties with whatever partner country can offer the best deals. Fintech offers new and more efficient methods to make financial transactions across borders. Over time, as some political divisions diminish while others appear, firms that face restrictions on their global activity will seek new ways of doing business and making profits in new venues. The sources of international investment income will change as capital flows are reoriented to new areas and perhaps take new forms.

Appendix

Advanced Economies		
Australia	Germany	Portugal
Austria	Greece	Spain
Canada	Italy	Sweden
Denmark	Japan	United Kingdom
Finland	New Zealand	United States
France	Norway	

Emerging Market Economies		
Argentina	Indonesia	Poland
Chile	Latvia	Russia
Colombia	Lithuania	Slovak Republic
Czech Republic	Malaysia	South Africa
Egypt	Mexico	South Korea
Estonia	Pakistan	Thailand
Hungary	Peru	
India	Philippines	

References

Accominotti, O. and Eichengreen, B. (2016). The Mother of All Sudden Stops: Capital Flows and Reversals in Europe, 1919–32. *Economic History Review*, 69(2), 496–492.

Acosta, P. A., Lartey, E. K. K., and Mandelman, F. S. (2009). Remittances and the Dutch Disease. *Journal of International Economics*, 79(1), 102–116.

Afram, G. G. (2012). *The Remittance Market in India*. Washington, DC: World Bank.

Ajami, R. A. and Karimi, K. A. (2023). Sovereign Wealth Funds: Opportunities, Global Challenges and Relevance to the Oil-Producing Economies. *Journal of Asia-Pacific Business*, 24(3), 145–148.

Alberola, A., Estrada, Á., and Viani, F. (2020). Global Imbalances from a Stock Perspective: The Asymmetry between Creditors and Debtors. *Journal of International Money and Finance*, 107, 1–20.

Almadani, S., Batty, M., Nemschoff, D., and Passmore, S. W. (2020). The Stability of Safe Asset Production. FEDS Notes No. November 9, 2020. https://doi.org/10.17016/2380-7172.2787.

Amighini, A. A., McMillan, M., and Sanfilippo, M. (2017). FDI and Capital Formation in Developing Economies: New Evidence from Industry-Level Data, NBER Working Paper no. 23049. Cambridge, MA: National Bureau of Economic Research.

Amuedo-Dorantes, C. and Pozo, S. (2023). *The Widespread Impacts of Remittance Flows*. Institute of Labor Economics (IZA), pp. 1–97.

Attig, N., Guedhami, O., Nazaire, G., and Sy, O. (2023). What Explains the Benefits of International Portfolio Diversification? *Journal of International Financial Markets, Institutions & Money*, 83, 1–15.

Avdjiev, S., Everett, M., Lane, P. R., and Shin, H. S. (2018). Tracking the International Footprints of Global Firms. *BIS Quarterly Review*, March, 47–66.

Aysun, U. and Hepp, R. (2016). The Determinants of Global Bank Lending: Evidence from Bilateral Cross-Country Data. *Journal of Banking & Finance*, 66, 35–52.

Badger, D. G. (1951). The Balance of Payments: A Tool of Economic Analysis. *IMF Staff Papers*, 2(1), 86–197.

Baele, L., Pungulescu, C., and Ter Horst, J. (2007). Model Uncertainty, Financial Market Integration and the Home Bias Puzzle. *Journal of International Money and Finance*, 26(4), 606–630.

Balcao Reis, A. B. (2001). On the Welfare Effects of Foreign Investments. *Journal of International Economics*, 54(2), 411–427.

Baldwin, R. (2016). *The Great Convergence: Information Technology and the New Globalization*. Cambridge, MA: Harvard University Press.

Baldwin, R. and Freeman, R. (2021). Risks and Global Supply Chains: What We Know and What We Need to Know. NBER Working Paper no. 29444. Cambridge, MA: National Bureau of Economic Research.

Balli, F., Basher, S. A., and Ozer Balli, H. (2011). Income Insurance and the Determinants of Income Insurance via Foreign Asset Revenues and Foreign Liability Payments. *Economic Modeling*, 25(5), 203–213.

Balli, F., Basher, S. A., and Ozer Balli, H. (2013). International Income Risk Sharing and the Global Financial Crisis of 2008–2009. *Journal of Banking and Finance*, 37(7), 203–213.

Banerjee, B. (2020). Digital Currencies and Cross-Border Policy Cooperation and Coordination. *G20 Digest*, 2, 23–34.

Bang, J. T. and MacDermott, R. (2019). Does FDI Attract Immigrants? An Empirical Gravity Model Approach. *International Migration Review*, 53(1), 237–253.

Behar, A. and Hassan, R. (2022). The Current Account Income Balance: External Adjustment Channel or Vulnerability Amplifier? IMF Working Paper no. 2022/106. Washington, DC: International Monetary Fund.

Bénétrix, A., Lane, P. R., and Shambaugh, J. C. (2015). International Currency Exposures, Valuation Effects and the Global Financial Crisis. *Journal of International Economics*, 96, S98–S109.

Bertaut, C., Bressler, B., and Curcuru, S. (2018). Globalization and the Geography of Capital Flows. Ninth IFC Conference. Basel: Bank for International Settlements.

Bolt, W., de Haan, L., Hoeberichts, M., van Oordt, M. R. C., and Swank, J. (2012). Bank Profitability during Recessions. *Journal of Banking & Finance*, 36(9), 2552–2564.

Boonman, T. M. (2023). Portfolio Capital Flows before and after the Global Financial Crisis. *Economic Modelling*, 127, 1–17.

Boughton, J. M. (2012). *Tearing Down Walls*. Washington, DC: IMF.

Bracke, T. and Schmitz, M. (2011). Channels of International Risk-sharing: Capital Gains versus Income Flows. *International Economics and Economic Policy*, 8(1), 45–78.

Broto, C., Diaz-Cassou, J., and Erce, A. (2011). Measuring and Explaining the Volatility of Capital Flows to Emerging Countries. *Journal of Banking & Finance*, 35(8), 1941–1953.

Buch, C. M. (2005). Distance and International Banking. *Review of International Economics*, 13(4), 787–804.

Buch, C. M. and Kuckulenz, A. (2009). Worker Remittances and Capital Flows to Developing Countries. *International Migration*, 48(5), 89–117.

Bugamelli, M. and Paterno, F. (2009). Do Workers' Remittances Reduce the Probability of Current Account Reversals? *World Development*, 37(12), 1821–1838.

Calvo, G. (1998). Capital Flows and Capital-Market Crises: The Simple Economics of Sudden Stops. *Journal of Applied Economics*, 1(1), 35–54.

Capelli, C. and Vaggi, G. (2016). Why Gross National Disposable Income Should Replace Gross National Income. *Development and Change*, 47(2), 223–239.

Carling, J. (2008). The Determinants of Migrant Remittances. *Oxford Review of Economic Policy*, 24(3), 581–598.

Carrera, J., Montes-Roja, G., Panigo, D., and Toledo, F. (2024). Income Inequality and External Wealth of Nations. *Journal of Globalization and Development*, 15(1), 47–62. https://doi.org/10.1515/jgd-2023-0042.

Casella, B., Borga, M., and Wacker, K. M. (2023). Measuring Multinational Production with Foreign Direct Investment Statistics: Recent Trends, Challenges and Developments. IMF Working Paper no. 23/12. Washington, DC: IMF.

Cavallo, E., Powell, A., Pedemonte, M., and Tavella, P. A. (2015). A New Taxonomy of Sudden Stops: Which Sudden Stops Should Countries Be Most Concerned about? *Journal of International Money and Finance*, 51, 47–70.

Cazachevici, A., Havranek, T., and Horvath, R. (2020). Remittances and Economic Growth. *World Development*, 134.

Chakravarty, S. and Xiang, M. (2011). Determinants of Profit Reinvestment by Small Businesses in Emerging Economies. *Financial Management*, 40(3), 63–82.

Chami, R., Barajas, A., Cosimano, T. et al. (2008). Macroeconomic Consequences of Remittances. Occasional Paper 259, Washington, DC: IMF.

Chen, S.-H. and Liao, C.-C. (2011). Are Foreign Banks More Profitable than Domestic Banks? Home- and Host-Country Effects of Banking Market Structure, Governance, and Supervision. *Journal of Banking & Finance*, 35(4), 819–839.

Chen, W., Mrkaic, M., and Nabar, M. S. (2019). The Global Economic Recovery 10 Years after the 2008 Financial Crisis. IMF Working Paper no. 19/83. Washington, DC: IMF.

Claessens, S. (2017). Global Banking: Recent Developments and Insights from Research. *Review of Finance*, 21(4), 1513–1555.

Claessens, S. and van Horen, N. (2013). Impact of Foreign Banks. *Journal of Financial Perspectives*, 1(1), 29–42.

Clarke, H. (1995). International Labor-cum Capital Migrations: Theory, Welfare Implications, and Evidence. *Economies Review*, 6(4), 323–340.

Clausing, K. A. (2018). Does Tax Drive the Headquarters Locations of the World's Biggest Companies? *Transnational Corporations*, 25(2), 37–65.

Coeurdacier, N. and Guibard, S. (2011). International Portfolio Diversification Is Better than You Think. *Journal of International Money and Finance*, 30(2), 289–308.

Colacelli, M., Gautam, D., and Rebillard, C. (2021). Japan's Foreign Assets and Liabilities: Implications for the External Accounts. IMF Working Paper no. 21/26. Washington, DC: IMF.

Committee on the Global Financial System. (2021). Changing Patterns of Capital Flows. CGFS Paper no. 66. Basel: Bank for International Settlements.

Coppola, A., Maggiro, M., Neiman, B., and Schreger. A. (2021). Redrawing the Map of Global Capital Flows: The Role of Cross-Border Financing and Tax Haven. *Quarterly Journal of Economics*, 136(3), 1499–1556.

Damgaard, J., Elkjaer, T., and Johannesen, N. (2024). What Is Real and What Is Not in the Global FDI Network? *Journal of International Money and Finance*, 140, 1–25. https://doi.org/10.1016/j.jimonfin.2023.102971.

Daude, C. and Fratzscher, M. (2008). The Pecking Order of Cross-Border Investment. *Journal of International Economics*, 74(1), 94–119.

De, S., Islamaj, E., Kose, M. A., and Yousefi, S. R. (2019). Remittances over the Business Cycle: Theory and Evidence. *Economic Notes*, 48(3), 1–18.

De Beer, B. and Rangasamy, L. (2015). Some Impacts of South African FDI Flows on the Current Account Balance. *Journal for Studies in Economics and Econometrics*, 39(1), 99–116.

Di Vito, L., Fuentes, F. M., and Leite, J. M. (2023). Understanding the Profitability Gap between Euro Area and US Globally Systemically Important Banks. ECB Occasional Paper no. 327. Frankfurt: European Central Bank.

Doeswijk, R., Lam, T., and Swinkels, L. (2020). Historical Returns of the Market Portfolio. *Review of Asset Pricing Studies*, 10, 521–567.

Donato, G. and Tille, C. (2024). International Investment Income: Patterns, Drivers, and Heterogeneous Sensitivities. CEPR Discussion Paper No. 19251. London: CEPR Press. https://cepr.org/publications/dp19251.

Driessen, J. and Laeven, L. (2007). International Portfolio Diversification Benefits: Cross-Country Evidence from a Local Perspective. *Journal of Banking & Finance*, 31(6), 1693–1712.

Dunning, J. H. (2001). The Eclectic (OLI) Paradigm of International Production: Past, Present and Future. *International Journal of the Economics of Business*, 8(2), 173–190.

Dyreng, S. and Hanlon, M. (2021). Tax Avoidance and Multinational Firm Behavior. In Fritz C. Foley, J. Hines, Jr., and D. Wessel, eds., *Global Goliaths: Multinational Corporations in the 21st Century Economy*. Washington, DC: Brookings Institution Press, pp. 361–435.

Edelstein, M. (1976). Realized Rates of Return on U.K. Home and Overseas Portfolio Investment in the Age of High Imperialism. *Explorations in Economic History*, 13(3), 283–329.

Edelstein, M. (1982). *Overseas Investment in the Age of High Imperialism: The United Kingdom, 1850–1914*. New York: Columbia University Press.

Eichengreen, B. (2015). *Hall of Mirrors: The Great Depression, the Great Recession, and the Uses-and Misuses-of History*. Oxford: Oxford University Press.

Eichengreen, B. (2024). Globalization and Growth in a Bipolar World. Working Paper no. WP 161. New Delhi: National Council of Applied Economic Research.

Eichengreen, B. and Temin, P. (2000). The Gold Standard and the Great Depression. *Contemporary European History*, 9(2), 183–207.

Eichengreen, B., Csonto, B., and El-Gananiny, A. (2022). Financial Globalization. In V. Cerra, B. Eichengreen, A. El-Ganainy, and M. Schindler, eds., *How to Achieve Inclusive Growth*. Oxford: Oxford University Press, pp. 286–318.

Elizalde, H. (2008). The International Monetary Fund and Current Account Convertibility. In IMF, ed., *Current Developments in Monetary and Financial Law*. Washington, DC: IMF, pp. 17–40.

Esteves, R. and Khoudor-Castéras, D. (2009). A Fantastic Rain of Gold: European Migrants' Remittances and Balance of Payments Adjustment during the Gold Standard Period. *Journal of Economic History*, 69(4), 951–985.

Eugster, J. and Donato, G. (2022). The Exchange Rate Elasticity of the Swiss Current Account. SNB Working Paper 14/2022. Zurich: Swiss National Bank.

Feinstein, C. H. (1995). *Banking, Currency, and Finance in Europe in between the Wars*. Oxford and New York: Oxford University Press.

Findlay, R. and O'Rourke, K. H. (2007). *Power and Plenty: Trade, War, and the World Economy in the Second Millennium*. Princeton, NJ: Princeton University Press.

Fischer, A. M., Groeger, H., Sauré, P., and Yeşin, P. (2019). Current Account Adjustment and Retained Earnings. *Journal of International Money and Finance*. 94, 246–259.

Fisman, R. and Love, I. (2003). Trade Credit, Financial Intermediary Development, and Industry Growth. *Journal of Finance*, 58(1), 353–374.

Florez-Orrego, S., Maggiori, M., Schreger, J., Sun, Z., and Tinda, S. (2023). Global Capital Allocation. NBER Working Paper no. 31599. Cambridge, MA: NBER.

Forbes, K., Hjortse, I., and Nenova, T. (2017). Current Account Deficits during Heightened Risk: Menacing or Mitigating? *The Economic Journal*, 127(601), 571–627.

Freund, C. and Spatafora, N. (2008). Remittances, Transactions Costs, and Informality. *Journal of Development Economics*, 86(2), 356–366.

Fukuma, N., Morishita, K., and Nakamura, T. (2016). Recent Trends in Japan's Balance of Payments. *Bank of Japan Review*, no. 16-E-8. Tokyo: Bank of Japan.

Ganapati, S. and Wong, W. F. (2023). How Far Goods Travel: Global Transport and Supply Chains from 1965–2020. *Journal of Economic Perspectives*, 37(3), 3–30.

Garcia-Bernardo, J. and Jansky, P. (2021). Profit Shifting of Multinational Corporations Worldwide. IES Working Papers no. 14/2021. Prague: Institute of Economic Studies, Charles University.

Gechert, S., Havranek, T., Irsova, Z., and Kolcunova, D. (2022). Measuring Capital-Labor Substitution: The Importance of Method Choices and Publication Bias. *Review of Economic Dynamics*, 45, 55–82.

Gertner, R. H., Scharfstein, D. S., and Stein., J. C. (1994). Internal versus External Capital Markets. *Quarterly Journal of Economics*, 109(4), 1211–1230.

Gethin, A. (2018). Foreign Income and Assets in Comparative Perspective: Highlights from the World Inequality Database. WID. World Issue Brief. Paris: World Inequality Lab.

Gheasi, M., Nijkamp, P., and Rietveld, P. (2011). Migrants and International Economic Linkages: A Meta-Overview. *Spatial Economic Analysis*, 6(4), 359–376.

Goetzmann, W. N. (2017). *Money Changes Everything*. Princeton, NJ: Princeton University Press.

Goldstein, I. and Razin, A. (2006). An Information-Based Trade Off between Foreign Direct Investment and Foreign Portfolio Investment. *Journal of International Economics*, 70(1), 271–295.

Gopinath, G., Gourinchas, P.-O., Presbitero, A., and Topalova, P. (2024). Changing Global Linkages: A New Cold War? Working Paper 24/76. Washington, DC: IMF.

Gou, Q., Li, X., and Zhao, G. (2024). Surges of Cross Border Capital Flow: The Impact of Digital Finance. *Pacific-Basin Finance Journal*, 84.

Graff, M., Kenwood, A. G., and Lougheed, A. L. (2014). *Growth of the International Economy, 1820–2015*. Abingdon-on-Thames: Routledge.

Hansen, E. and Wagner, R. (2022). The Reinvestment by Multinationals as a Capital Flow: Crises, Imbalances and the Cash-Based Current Account. *Journal of International Money and Finance*, 124.

Hassan, G. M. and Holmes, M. J. (2016). Do Remittances Facilitate a Sustainable Current Account? *World Economy*, 39(11), 1934–1853.

Hatayama, M. (2019). *The Role of Regional Financial Centres for Development Finance*. K4D Helpdesk Report 522. Brighton: Institute of Development Studies.

Hattari, R. and Rajan, R. S. (2011). How Different Are FDI and FPI Flows? Distance and Capital Market Integration. *Journal of Economic Integration*, 26(3), 499–525.

Hatton, T. J. and Williamson, J. G. (2008). *Global Migration and the World Economy: Two Centuries of Policy and Performance*. Cambridge, MA: MIT Press.

Heimberger, P. (2020). Does Economic Globalisation Affect Income Inequality? A Meta-analysis. *The World Economy*, 43(1), 2960–2982.

High, J. (2000). Balance of Payments. In K. Reinert, R. Rajan, A. Glass, and L. S. Davis, eds., *The Princeton Encyclopedia of the World Economy*. Princeton, NJ: Princeton University Press, pp. 102–107.

Hobson, J. (1902). *Imperialism, a Study*. New York: James Pott.

Hufbauer, G. C. and Adler, M. B. (2010). The Rise of Emerging Market Multinationals: Economic and Business Challenges Ahead. In K. P. Sauvant, G. McAllister, and W. A. Maschek, eds., *Foreign Direct Investments from Emerging Markets*. New York: Palgrave Macmillan, pp. 413–424.

Hünnekes, F., Konradt, M., Schularick, M., Trebesch, C., and Wingenbach, J. (2023). Exportweltmeister: Germany's Foreign Investment Returns in International Comparison. International Economics Department Working Paper no. HEIDWP03-2023. Geneva: Graduate Institute of International and Development Studies.

IMF. (2013). *Balance of Payments and International Investment Manual. 6th ed*. Washington, DC: IMF.

IMF. (2018). *The Bali Fintech Agenda*. Washington, DC: IMF.

IMF. (2020). *Special Purpose Entities: Guidelines for a Data Template*. Washington, DC: IMF.

IMF. (2023). *World Economic Outlook*. April. Washington, DC: IMF.

IOM. (2022). *Essential of Migration Management v2.0 Handbook*. Geneva: International Organization for Migration, https://emm.iom.int/handbooks.

Islamaj, E. and Kose, A. K. (2022). What Types of Capital Flows Help Improve International Risk Sharing? *Journal of International Money and Finance*, 122.

Johnson, R. C. (2014). Five Facts about Value-Added Exports and Implications for Macroeconomics and Trade Research. *Journal of Economic Perspectives*, 28(2), 119–142.

Jones, G. (2005). *Multinationals and Global Capitalism*. Oxford: Oxford University Press.

Joyce, J. P. (2019). Partners, Not Debtors: The External Liabilities of Emerging Market Economies. *Journal of Economic Behavior & Organization*, 157, 320–337.

Joyce, J. P. (2021). The Sources of International Investment Income in Emerging Market Economies. *Review of International Economics*, 29(3), 606–625.

Joyce, J. P. (2024). The Impact of FDI Income on Income Shares in Home Countries. *Journal of Economic Inequality*, 22(2), 265–284.

Keller, W. and Olney, W. W. (2021). Globalization and Executive Compensation. *Journal of International Economics*, 129.

Keynes, J. M. (1920). *The Economic Consequences of the Peace*. New York: Harcourt, Brace and Howe.

Kindleberger, C. (1984). *A Financial History of Western Europe*. London: Allen & Unwin.

Klapper, L., Laeven, L., and Rajan, R. (2012). Trade Credit Contracts. *Review of Financial Studies*, 25(3), 838–867.

Knetsch, T. A. and Nagengast, A. J. (2017). Penny Wise and Pound Foolish? On the Income from Germany's Foreign Investments. *Review of World Economics*, 153(4), 753–778.

Kodongo, O. and Ojah, K. (2017). Equity Markets. In K. Reinert, ed., *Handbook of Globalisation and Development*. Cheltenham: Edward Elgar, pp. 201–217.

Koepke, R. (2019). What Drives Capital Flows to Emerging Markets? A Survey of the Empirical Literature. *Journal of Economic Surveys*, 33(2), 516–540.

Kose, M. A., Prasad, E. S., and Terrones, M. E. (2009). Does Financial Globalization Promote Risk Sharing? *Journal of Development Economics*, 89, 258–270.

Kosse, A. and Vermuelen, R. (2014). Migrants' Choice of Remittance Channel: Do General Payment Habits Play a Role? *World Development*, 62, 213–227.

Kua, B. L. (2019). Money by Mail to China: Qiaopi and Chinese Remittance in Singapore. In C. G. Kwa and B. L. Kua, eds., *A General History of the Chinese in Singapore*. Singapore: World Scientific, pp. 639–651.

Kugler, M. and Rapoport, H. (2007). International Labor and Capital Flows: Complements or Substitutes? *Economics Letters*, 94(2), 155–162.

Kugler, M., Levintal, O., and Rapoport, H. (2018). Migration and Cross-Border Financial Flows. *World Bank Economic Review*, 31(1), 148–162.

Kuwahata, H. (2023). The Impact of Foreign Direct Investment on Executive Compensation: Evidence from the Great Recession. *Applied Economic Letters*, 30(13), 1738–1743.

Lane, P. R. (2001). Do International Investment Income Flows Smooth Income? *Weltwirtschaftliches Archiv*, 137(2), 714–736.

Lane, P. R. (2015). A Financial Perspective on the UK Current Account Deficit. *National Economic Review*, 234(1), F67–F72.

Lane, P. R. and Milesi-Ferretti, G. M. (2018). The External Wealth of Nations Revisited: International Financial Integration in the Aftermath of the Global Financial Crisis. *IMF Economic Review*, 66(1), 189–122.

Langenmayr, D. and Li, L. (2023). Home or away? Profit Shifting with Territorial Taxation. *Journal of Public Economics*, 217.

Lartey, E. K. K. (2019). The Effect of Remittances on the Current Account in Developing and Emerging Economies. *Economic Notes*, 48(3), 1–17.

Lartey, E. K. K., Mandelbaum, F. S., and Acosta, P. A. (2012). Remittances, Exchange Rate Regimes and the Dutch Disease: A Panel Data Analysis. *Review of International Economics*, 20(2), 377–912.

Leblang, D. (2010). Familiarity Breeds Investment: Diaspora Networks and International Investment. *American Political Science Review*, 104(3), 584–600.

Lim, K. B. (2019). Money by Mail to China: Qiaopi and Chinese Remittance in Singapore. In K. C. Guan and K. B. Lim, eds., *A General History of the Chinese in Singapore*. Singapore: World Scientific, pp. 637–650.

Lipsey, R. E. (2003). Foreign Direct Investment and the Operations of Multinational Firms: Concepts, History and Data. In E. K. Choi and J. Harrigan, eds., *Handbook of International Trade*, Malden, MA: Blackwell, pp. 287–319.

Lipsey, R. E., Feenstra, R. C., Hahn, C. H., and Hatsopoulos, G. N. (1999). The Role of Foreign Direct Investment in International Capital Flows. In M. Feldstein, ed., *International Capital Flows*. Chicago: University of Chicago Press, pp. 307–331.

Ma, L. and Ruzic. D. (2020). Globalization and Top Income Shares. *Journal of International Economics*, 125.

McCauley, R.N., McGuire, P., and Wooldridge, P. (2021) Seven Decades of International Banking. *BIS Quarterly Review,* September, 61–75.

Machokoto, M., Gyimah, D., and Ibrahim, B. M. (2022). The Evolution of Trade Credit: New Evidence from Developed versus Developing Countries. *Review of Quantitative Finance and Accounting*, 59(3), 857–912.

Mills, G. (1994). Early Accounting in Northern Italy: The Role of Commercial Development and the Printing Press in the Expansion of Double-Entry from Genoa, Florence and Venice. *Accounting Historians Journal*, 21(1), 81–96.

Mundell, R. (1957). International Trade and Factor Mobility. *American Economic Review*, 47(3), 321–335.

Mundell, R. A. (1963). Capital Mobility and Stabilization Policy under Fixed and Flexible Exchange Rates. *Canadian Journal of Economics and Political Science*, 29(4), 475–485.

Myers, C. and Majluf, N. S. (1984). Corporate Financing and Investment Decisions When Firms Have Information That Investors Do Not Have. *Journal of Financial Economics*, 13(2), 187–221.

O'Rourke, K. H. and Williamson, J. G. (1999). *Globalization and History: The Evolution of a Nineteenth-Century Atlantic Economy*. Cambridge, MA: MIT Press.

Obstfeld, M. and Taylor, A. M. (2004). *Global Capital Markets: Integration, Crisis, and Growth*. Cambridge, MA: Cambridge University Press.

OECD. (2015). *How Multinational Enterprises Channel Investments Through Multiple Countries*. Paris: OECD.

OECD. (2022). *FDI in Figures*, October. Paris: OECD.

OECD. (2023). *Economic Impact Assessment of the Two Pillar Solution*. Paris: OECD.

OECD. (2024). *FDI in Figures*. April. Paris: OECD.

Oseghale, B. D. and Nwachukwu, O. C. (2010). Effect of the Quality of Host Country Institutions on Reinvestments by United States Multinationals: A Panel Data Analysis. *International Journal of Management*, 27(3), 497–510.

Pagliari, M. S. and Swarnali, A. H. (2024). The Volatility of Capital Flows in Emerging Markets: Measures and Determinants. *Journal of International Money and Finance*, 145.

Papaioannou, E. (2009). What Drives International Financial Flows? Politics, Institutions and Other Determinants. *Journal of Development Economics*, 88(2), 269–281.

Petersen, M. A. and Rajan, R. G. (1997). Trade Credit: Theories and Evidence. *Review of Financial Studies*, 10(3), 661–691.

Piketty, T. (2014). *Capital in the Twenty-First Century.* Cambridge, MA: Harvard University Press.

Pizzola, B. and Carroll, R. J. (2024). Decades-long Decline in FG500 Companies Headquartered in US Has Reversed. *Bloomberg Daily Tax Report.* EY. https://news.bloombergtax.com/daily-tax-report/the-changing-headquarters-landscape-for-fortune-global-500-companies.

Polat, B. (2017). Determinants of Reinvested Earnings as a Component of Foreign Direct Investment. *Journal of Economics and Management Research*, 6(1), 24–45.

Ramirez, M. D. (2011). Is Foreign Direct Investment Productive in the Latin American Case? A Panel Co-Integration Analysis, 1980–2002. *International Trade Journal*, 25(1), 35–72.

Ratha, D., Plaza, S., Kim, E. J. et al. (2023). *Migration and Development Brief 38: Remittances Remain Resilient but Are Slowing.* Washington, DC: KNOMAD-World Bank.

Reinert, K. (2021). Mercantilism. In P. James, ed., *Oxford Bibliographies in International Relations*. Oxford: Oxford University Press.

Reinhart, C. M. and Rogoff, K. S. (2009). *This Times Is Different: Eight Centuries of Financial Folly.* Princeton, NJ: Princeton University Press.

Rogoff, K. S. and Tashiro, T. (2015). Japan's Exorbitant Privilege. *Journal of the Japanese and International Economies*, 35, 43–61.

Salter, A. (1951). *Foreign Investment.* Princeton, NJ: Princeton University.

Sanderson, M. R. and Kentor, J. (2008). Foreign Direct Investment and International Migration: A Cross-National Analysis of Less-Developed Countries, 1985–2000. *International Sociology*, 23(4), 514–539.

Sarno, L., Tsiakas, I., and Ulloa, B. (2016). What Drives International Portfolio Flows? *Journal of International Money and Finance*, 60, 53–72.

Schroth, J. (2023). Capital Flows and Growth across Developing Countries. *Journal of International Money and Finance*, 137.

Sengupta, R. and Noeth, B. J. (2012). Emerging Markets: A Source of and Destination for Capital. *The Regional Economist*, 12(1), 10–11.

Shirota, T. (2015). What Is the Major Determinant of Cross-Border Flows? *Journal of International Money and Finance*, 53, 137–147.

Shiroyama, T. (2019). Overseas Chinese Remittances in the Mid-Twentieth Century. In C. Choi, T. Shiroyama, and T. Oishi, eds., *Chinese and Indian Merchants in Modern Asia*. Leiden, NL: Brill, pp. 72–103.

Siebert, H. (2002). *The World Economy* (2nd ed.). Abingdon-on-Thames: Routledge.

Solimano, A. and Watts, N. (2005). International Migration, Capital Flows and the Global Economy: A Long Run View. *Macroeconomía del Desarrollo* series 35. Santiago: United Nations.

Sørenson, B., Wu, Y.-T., Yosha, O., and Zhu, Y. (2007). Home Bias and International Risk Sharing: Twin Puzzles Separated at Birth. *Journal of International Money and Finance*, 26(4), 587–605.

Strauss, I. (2018). Explaining Global Trends in FDI in 2015 and beyond. In L. E. Sachs and L. Johnson, eds., *Yearbook on International Investment Law and Policy 2015–2016*. Oxford: Oxford University Press, pp. 3–41.

Temesvary, J. (2014). The Determinants of U.S. Banks International Activities. *Journal of Banking and Finance*, 44, 233–247.

Temesvary, J. and Banai, A. (2017). The Drivers of Foreign Bank Lending in Central and Eastern Europe: The Roles of Parent, Subsidiary and Host Market Traits. *Journal of International Money and Finance*, 77, 157–173.

Tesar, L. L. (1993). International Risk Sharing and Non-traded Goods. *Journal of International Economics*, 26, 587–605.

The Economist. (2024). Chinese Firms Are Growing Rapidly in the Global South. August 1, 2024.

Tille, C. and Donato, G. (2023). International Investment Income: Patterns, Drivers, and Heterogeneous Sensitivities. IMF Research Conference. Washington, DC: IMF.

Tørsløv, T., Wier, L., and Zucman, G. (2023). The Missing Profits of Nations. *Review of Economic Studies*, 90(3), 1499–1534.

UNCTAD. (2022). *World Investment Report 2022*. New York: United Nations.

UNCTAD. (2024). *Global Economic Fracturing and Shifting Investment Patterns*. Geneva: UNCTAD.

United Nations. (2020). *International Migration Report 2020*. New York: United Nations.

Vicard, V. (2023). Profits Shifting, Returns of Foreign Direct Investments and Investment Income Imbalances. *IMF Economic Review*, 71(2), 369–414.

Wacker, K. M. (2024). Investment Incomes vs. the Trade Balance: Is the Current Account Still a Meaningful Concept. Oesterreichische NationalBank Working Paper no. 256. Vienna: Oesterreichische NationalBank.

Wier, L. and Zucman, G. (2022). Global Profit Shifting, 1975–2019. WIDER Working Paper no. 2022/121. Helsinki: United National Institute World Institute for Development Economics Research.

Wilner, B. S. (2000). The Exploitation of Relationships in Financial Distress: The Case of Trade Credit. *Journal of Finance*, 55(1), 153–178.

Wolff, E. N. (2021). Household Wealth Trends in the United States, 1962 to 2019: Median Wealth Rebounds . . . but Not Enough. NBER Working Paper no. 28383. Cambridge, MA: National Bureau of Economic Research.

Xu, T., Hu, K., and Das, U. (2019). U.S. Bank Profitability and Financial Stability. IMF Working Paper no, 19/5. Washington, DC: International Monetary Fund.

Yakubovskiy, S. A., Rodionova, T. A., and Derkach, T. V. (2019). Impact of Foreign Investment Income on External Positions of Emerging Market Economies. *Transition Studies Review*, 26(1), 71–81.

Yang, D. (2011). Migrant Remittances. *Journal of Economic Perspectives*, 25(3), 129–152.

Zélity, B. (2022). The Welfare Effects of FDI: A Quantitative Analysis. *Journal of Comparative Economics*, 50(1), 293–320.

Zélity, B. (2024). The Determinants of FDI Reinvestment Rates. *Open Economies Review*, https://doi.org/10.1007/s11079-024-09763-8.

Zucman, G. (2019). Global Wealth Inequality. *Annual Review of Economics*, 11, 109–113.

Acknowledgments

I am grateful to several Wellesley College women who provided research assistance: Mary Feser '20, Tyler Neri '25, and Audrey Wang '27. Rebecca Pocase of the U.S. Bureau of Economic Analysis gave valuable technical assistance, and Astrit Sulstarova of UNCTAD supplied data. I greatly benefited from the guidance of Ken Reinert, editor of the International Economics series of *Cambridge Elements*, who gave me the opportunity to write this Element. Two anonymous referees offered valuable suggestions.

Cambridge Elements ≡

International Economics

Kenneth A. Reinert
George Mason University

Kenneth A. Reinert is Professor of Public Policy in the Schar School of Policy and Government at George Mason University where he directs the Global Commerce and Policy master's degree program. He is author of *An Introduction to International Economics: New Perspectives on the World Economy* with Cambridge University Press and coauthor of *Globalization for Development: Meeting New Challenges* with Oxford University Press. He is also editor of *The Handbook of Globalisation and Development* with Edward Elgar and co-editor of the two-volume *Princeton Encyclopedia of the World Economy* with Princeton University Press.

About the Series

International economics is a distinct field with both fundamental theoretical insights and increasing empirical and policy relevance. The *Cambridge Elements in International Economics* showcases this field, covering the subfields of international trade, international money and finance, and international production, and featuring both established researchers and new contributors from all parts of the world. It aims for a level of theoretical discourse slightly above that of the *Journal of Economic Perspectives* to maintain accessibility. It extends Cambridge University Press' established reputation in international economics into the new, digital format of *Cambridge Elements*. It attempts to fill the niche once occupied by the *Princeton Essays in International Finance*, a series that no longer exists.

There is a great deal of important work that takes place in international economics that is set out in highly theoretical and mathematical terms. This new Elements does not eschew this work but seeks a broader audience that includes academic economists and researchers, including those working in international organizations, such as the World Bank, the International Monetary Fund, and the Organization for Economic Cooperation and Development.

Cambridge Elements $\equiv$

International Economics

Elements in the Series

www.ingramcontent.com/pod-product-compliance
Ingram Content Group UK Ltd.
Pitfield, Milton Keynes, MK11 3LW, UK
UKHW021842030325
455810UK00016B/771